Contents

Brother to Brother

The story of the Latter-day Saint missionaries
who took the gospel to Black Africa

Rendell N. Mabey
and
Gordon T. Allred

Bookcraft
Salt Lake City, Utah

Library of Congress Catalog Card Number: 84-70066
ISBN O-88494-519-7

2 3 4 5 6 7 8 9 10   89 88 87 86 85

Lithographed in the United States of America
PUBLISHERS PRESS
Salt Lake City, Utah

Preface

I first met Rendell Mabey in 1962, when we collaborated on an article about one of his lion hunts in Africa some years before. I had no idea then that the two of us would eventually write a book involving a far more significant experience in the same continent—his remarkable year as leader of the first group of Latter-day Saint missionaries to Black Africa.

Prior to that particular call, Rendell N. Mabey—prominent businessman and attorney from Bountiful, Utah—had already served as stake president, Regional Representative, and president of the Swiss Mission. In addition, he knew the ways of Africa well, having been there often on safari and on various business enterprises. Obviously he was an excellent choice for such a challenging undertaking.

That the Lord used him and his missionary associates to good purpose is clear from the results. Hundreds upon hundreds of people were eagerly awaiting the opportunity for baptism. In that single, one-year mission, 1,723 black Africans joined the Church, and five districts and thirty-five branches were organized. It is truly a thrilling account, filled with human interest and suspense.

The story is told in this book through Rendell Mabey's eyes. It is derived from extensive interviews with him, helpful input from his wife, Rachel (his constant companion in that great adventure), and the detailed records he kept. Despite the rigorous, often dangerous demands of their existence, despite his seventy-one years and a heart problem (since remedied), he wrote an amazing 1,305 pages in his personal journals during that time. The entries, unfailingly made at the end of long, laborious days or in the early hours of morning, were recorded with meticulous care and marked sensitivity.

The challenge of distilling such a wealth of experience into the compass of this book while attempting to provide the needed emotional and creative flow has been both difficult and highly fulfilling. Working with Ren (as he is fondly known by friends) has been rewarding in many ways—above all because of the cooperation, hospitality, and love I have enjoyed in the Mabey home, and the friendship that follows.

Brother to Brother portrays a unique and inspiring experience. It is presented with the hope that it will strengthen testimony and the cause of missionary work everywhere and that it will foster appreciation and love among Latter-day Saints and all those they encounter throughout the world, regardless of racial or cultural differences.

GORDON T. ALLRED

CHAPTER ONE

Welcome and Welcome!

"Hang on!" someone warned. For an instant we were airborne as the taxi careened over a tooth-jarring strip of washboard and descended into the swale ahead. It was a hot day as usual, sweltering inside the cab even with the windows open, and the road was murderous. An irregular trail of red sand and billowing, choking dust, it was rutted and booby-trapped with chuckholes. Negotiating that road, in fact, was a bit like skidding along through snow, but our native driver handled it all with remarkable abandon.

"If only we had a little rain to cool things off," Rachel said. "Anything to get some relief from this heat."

"Rainy season's coming up," Ted reminded her. "Once that happens we'll be getting more water than we bargained for."

Sitting there in front next to the window, I laughed a bit wearily, leaned forward to free the shirt from my sweating back, and grabbed for the dash as we jolted over another chuckhole. "By then we may need to navigate these roads in a speedboat." Rachel, my wife of forty-five years, was in the back with our companions Edwin Q. (Ted) Cannon, Jr., and his wife, Janath. To my left was E. D. Ukwat, better known as Daniel—our newfound guide, interpreter, devoted friend, and

Rendell and Rachel Mabey in Accra, Ghana, early in their mission.

investigator. His skin, like the driver's, was very dark, and his forehead was beaded with perspiration. As usual, however, despite the growing discomfort, he was smiling and full of cheer.

"Sometimes we really need a boat in this country," Daniel grinned.

That morning, in fact, we had embarked from Calabar in a fast open boat with an outboard motor, traversing the mighty Cross River near its mouth in a one-hour journey to Oron. There we had hired the taxi and continued our quest, often with only the vaguest sense of direction. Addresses in that locale were nonexistent—merely the primitive-sounding names of tiny villages like Idung Imoh, Oding, Anang, and Okom . . . merely the knowledge that they were somewhere out there, people who were patiently waiting, who had been waiting throughout the years and praying for a miracle.

It was difficult at the moment to comprehend that we were a part of that miracle even though our efforts of the day had already met with gratifying success. For now, it was simply a matter of keeping body, soul, and vehicle together. Rounding a bend at one point, we narrowly escaped head-on collision with a truck. The road was hardly designed for two-way traffic, and driver's education was clearly not top priority in Nigeria, facts well attested to by the number of demolished vehicles along the wayside.

By now, however, we were encountering a few more natives, either cycling or afoot, and another small settlement had materialized. "Village Isighe," Daniel said. He smiled, displaying a set of prominent white teeth. "This is it—the one we've been looking for!"

All of us craned our necks, peering and exclaiming with surprise and relief. Just off the road was a rectangular white sign with neat block letters spelling: "Church of Jesus Christ of Latter-day Saints, Inc." The name of the village was just beneath. "And there, if I'm not mistaken," Ted said moments later, "is the chapel."

"That's it, all right," I agreed, "practically in our laps." Only fifty or sixty feet away was a primitive little meeting-house plastered with dried mud: hardly likely to win any prizes in architecture or to insure cool and comfort in such weather, but a literal delight to behold even so.

It was now one o'clock Saturday afternoon, but a good many people were leaving the premises, filing from the doorway and wandering down the little lanes much as though they had just completed a sacrament meeting. Men, women, and children all dressed in their Sunday best, some in white, others in exotic colors, were passing by as we left the taxi. A number had stopped, in fact, to stare. Their dark, lustrous eyes were full of wonderment, and some of them seemed too astonished to return our words of greeting.

"I wonder what's going on," Janath said. "Church meetings on Saturday?" Daniel smiled and shrugged, shaking his head, but it soon appeared that he was not a total stranger there.

"Some kind of meeting, obviously," I said. Even more obviously, we had just discovered another of those self-styled branches of the Church, growing independently for now like slips from the wild olive. More people who had learned about the gospel from an article in the *Reader's Digest,* letters to Salt Lake City, tracts, occasional copies of the Book of Mormon, or a passing visitor. Such congregations understood certain important principles of the restored gospel in most cases, enough to hunger and thirst for more, but their knowledge was meager and primitive. Their church meetings, in particular, bore little resemblance to those which had become such a fundamental pattern in our own lives and which we had long simply taken for granted.

Moments after leaving our taxi, we were greeted by several men in colorful native robes, clearly religious leaders of some kind. Foremost among them was a wiry little man who introduced himself as Evangelist B. J. Ekong, head of the so-called LDS churches in Isighe and several other villages of that general area. His eyes were alert, full of intense expectation, and he smiled radiantly as though the purpose of our visit had already been revealed. "How truly wonderful!" he exclaimed, and he began seizing our hands. "Praise be to the Lord! Welcome! welcome!"

We had anticipated a cordial welcome, certainly hoped for one, but nothing quite like this. For a moment it was hard to find an appropriate reply. "Well, we're very happy to be here," Ted said. "Looks as though you've just been holding a meeting of some kind."

"Yes, yes indeed," came the reply. Those with him nodded, beaming as though they shared some marvelous secret. "We must go ring the bell and summon our people to return immediately!"

"Oh, I don't think that's necessary for the moment," I began, but the Evangelist was irrepressible; all of them were filled with the same explosive spirit.

"Ah, but you don't quite understand," he persisted. "We really must ring the bell! The members of this congregation have been waiting for years. They have just completed a twenty-four-hour fast, praying to the Lord that his missionaries would come."

It is impossible to articulate the feelings of that moment, but the bell itself seemed full of rejoicing, and within minutes of our arrival we were seated in positions of honor before a congregation of approximately seventy-five people. All of them, even the smallest infants, seemed to observe our every movement and expression with fascination, and the Evangelist B. J. Ekong arose to offer his welcome in English.

"We have awaited this glad day for many years," he said, speaking in tones of great humility and dignity. "Now, very suddenly and without notice . . ." He hesitated, eyes glistening. "Now, very suddenly, you are here among us. You are here to bring that light and knowledge we so greatly desire and to show us the paths we must follow." He then turned to us more fully, making a slight bow and sweeping gesture with one hand. "For such a blessing we must thank our Father in Heaven everlastingly. Welcome, beloved and honored friends —welcome and welcome!"

I then arose as our senior representative and, with Daniel Ukwat to interpret, thanked all those present for their great devotion to the Lord, their interest and hospitality. "We have left our homes and employment, our families, and have journeyed halfway around the world to share with you the restored gospel in all its fulness," I said. "We bring you greetings from our prophet Spencer W. Kimball in Salt Lake City. We bring you word of his great love and prayers and are here today in that same spirit, convinced that we are all children of God and therefore literal brothers and sisters." I testified as well to the divinity of our Savior, explained briefly the mission of Joseph Smith, and bore witness of the fact that we were duly authorized representatives of the only true church upon this earth, an organization constantly sustained by the lifeblood of prophetic revelation.

It was without doubt a momentous experience, our arriving as we had "out of nowhere" much like aliens from another planet at the very conclusion of their fasting and prayers. Minutes before, we had not existed for them. Now we were here within their midst, products of an unknown culture with strange and pallid skins, speaking in what for most was a foreign tongue. Despite all this, however, and despite the necessity of an interpreter, we were "coming through." The Spirit of God, which in times of faith may transcend all other barriers, was bearing record. I could see it in their eyes and feel it in my veins, a conviction that steadily expanded as Elder Cannon and our wives in turn arose to unite their testimonies with my own. Last of all, Daniel himself attested to the fact that we were true messengers, divinely appointed to this mission.

At the conclusion of our remarks, various leaders from among the gathering arose to add their welcome and to ask questions. The heat was intense, and the entire congregation was seated on crude wooden benches, but no one wanted to leave. Above all else, they desired assurance that we had not come as mere birds of passage, that never again would they be left in the wilderness, comfortless and alone. "In time past," an old man said, "a member or two of your religion have appeared among us, but only for a fleeting moment. They brought us greetings in one breath and said farewell with the next. We were tempted with the truth only to have it snatched away again. No one returned, and our letters to Salt Lake City received little reply." His eyes smoldered, but the fire was quenched with tears. "Will it also be the same with you?"

I shook my head, finding it difficult to respond. "We can appreciate your feelings," I said, "and greatly regret that you have been kept waiting so long. It must have been a terrible frustration, but God has many ways of testing the faithful, and perhaps this has been one of them." I went on to explain that with the vast number of people in the world still waiting to hear our message, even the present 26,000 missionaries, nearly all of them self-supporting, were far from enough. "Many of them," I added, "must leave their jobs and professions in the hands of others as we have, but your prayers have been answered."

"Yes," Ted agreed. "This is the beginning. The restored gospel has come to Black Africa."

CHAPTER TWO

If the Call Should Come

I t was late morning, September 27, 1978, when the phone call came. I was completing some articles of incorporation in my Salt Lake City law office and was on the verge of leaving for lunch. "Ren?" the voice inquired. "This is Jim—Jim Faust."

"Well, Jim!" I intoned and felt the glow of recognition, a distinct sense of pleasure and anticipation. "How have you been?" Elder James E. Faust was then one of the presidents of the First Quorum of the Seventy and also president of the Church's International Mission, which includes parts of the world that currently do not lend themselves well to organized missions. We had been friends on a first-name basis for years, and our initial exchange was full of informality, all the conditioned questions and responses of old acquaintances who haven't seen each other for a while. But I felt the growing sense of inquiry that naturally arises at such times. Friends, yes, but why was he *really* calling? General Authorities of the Church are always tightly programmed, ever on the move; they rarely have time to "shoot the breeze."

"Ren," Elder Faust continued, "I'm calling at the request of the First Presidency. Would it be possible for you and Sister Mabey to meet in my office this afternoon at three-thirty?"

"Why, certainly," I replied. "Be happy to." Request of the First Presidency! Wife Rachel to be included! Now the question was all-consuming, but I absorbed the suspense to the best of my ability and was grateful for the only small favor possible—an early meeting and explanation. "Hope I haven't been a bad boy," I joked—just a little something to ease the pressure.

"No," he replied and chuckled. "You've been a *good* boy. See you at three-thirty."

There were five of us at that meeting: President Faust; Edwin Q. (Ted) Cannon, Jr., a counselor in the International Mission; David Kennedy, a world ambassador for the Church; Rachel; and myself. All of us were acquainted, in some cases friends of long standing, at ease with each other and happy to exchange pleasantries, to discuss the state of the Church and the world. Yet even so . . . I felt the growing excitement and sense of adventure along with relief when Elder Faust leaned forward in his chair and launched the explanation.

"Brother and Sister Mabey," he said, "we have invited you here today for the purpose of discussing a vital and challenging assignment, one very dear to the heart of our prophet. It's an assignment that will demand great determination and wisdom—above all, constant direction from the Spirit." He paused, looking rather solemn. "Not only that, but quite frankly, it will probably impose some real hardship. Consequently, for the moment at least, we're not really talking about an official call. This is simply a preliminary discussion."

"That's fine—we understand," I said, thinking how well he epitomized the determination and wisdom of which he spoke, noting the square, resolute jaw, the thick, graying hair, neatly parted in a straight line down the side. I looked at the others as well: David Kennedy, gracious and courtly with white hair like my own though rather full and flowing; Ted Cannon, with his memorable black-framed glasses, his round, youthful face ever cheerful and alert. There was an atmosphere of benign conspiracy about the whole thing.

Last of all, I looked at my wife, Rachel. She was seated beside me on the couch. The others faced us in chairs forming an intimate little circle. Her large hazel eyes were watchful but full of empathy and acceptance. "Well," I said, "you certainly have our attention."

President Faust smiled. "That's good, because it deserves all the attention we can muster." Then he leaned back and folded his arms. "As you probably know, there are a great many people in Black Africa, especially in Nigeria and Ghana, who have been longing and waiting for a long time to receive the restored gospel."

Africa! I felt a sudden tingling. *So that's what it's about!*

"Some of them have been requesting the missionaries for years now," he continued. "The first of these requests, in fact, began coming around 1959, and in 1963 four couples were actually called to serve as missionaries to Nigeria. Unfortunately, they were denied visas, and for various reasons the Church has maintained a hands-off policy ever since."

"A definite necessity," Elder Kennedy added, "but also a great discouragement for many of the good people over there."

"Yes, it certainly is," Elder Faust agreed. "Many of them had read about us in magazine articles and in certain cases managed to obtain some of our Church literature, including the Book of Mormon. As a result they have become impressed enough to organize branches of one sort or another on their own initiative, calling themselves The Church of Jesus Christ of Latter-day Saints. None of this has been authorized or accomplished through the power of the priesthood, and consequently they are Latter-day Saints in name only." He paused, reflecting. "Nevertheless, that gives you some idea of their tremendous interest and commitment."

"That's really amazing," Rachel exclaimed. "They must be a marvelous people."

"No doubt about it," came the reply, "but until now the time simply hasn't been ripe for direct proselyting, and during the interim a number of those organizations have pretty well dissolved." Again he paused. "That's the bad news. The good news is that times have changed. We have hopes that visas may now be available to both Nigeria and Ghana, and, even more importantly, the priesthood with its great saving ordinances is at last being granted to worthy male members of the Church everywhere, no matter what the color of their skins. One of the truly momentous revelations of this dispensation."

I could not have agreed more enthusiastically, and for several seconds I relived the feelings of that day only a few months before—June 8, 1978—when the announcement had come. Like so many others, I had been almost thunderstruck, yet filled with jubilation and immense relief. It was as though I too had emerged from bondage into the light. I cannot speak for our prophet, to whom that epoch-making revelation came, or those who were with him there in the temple, but the following by Elder Bruce R. McConkie seems very apt: ". . . the Lord in his providence poured out the Holy Ghost upon the First Presidency and the Twelve in a miraculous and marvelous manner, beyond anything that any then present had ever experienced."

Now, less than four months later, it appeared that my beloved wife and I were somehow becoming involved in the consequences of it all. An awesome moment, too sudden and stupendous for assimilation, but it was good to have her at my side.

During the ensuing discussion we learned that Ted Cannon and Merrill J. Bateman, Dean of Brigham Young University School of Business, had recently been sent on a two-week exploratory visit to Ghana and Nigeria, gathering much valuable information. "There are still about twenty so-called LDS congregations in Nigeria, totaling roughly two thousand people," Ted explained, "and approximately half that many in Ghana." There were also several actual Church members in both countries, foreigners residing there currently or natives who had been baptized while visiting other lands. Living conditions, Ted explained, were tough, even in the most civilized areas, and expenses outlandish.

"And, of course," Elder Kennedy explained, "our missionaries will have to protect their health constantly. Yellow fever, cholera, hepatitis, and malaria are still prevalent in many parts of West Africa." He shook his head. "Thank heaven for vaccines! But there are lots of problems, and medical facilities are hardly the best."

Elder Faust nodded, noting our reactions. "In some respects it will probably be a very lonely kind of mission also. That's one reason why we'll be sending married couples, at least initially, rather than young missionaries. As a matter of fact, we'll probably have two couples working together in a given area, partly to provide each other company and moral support."

"Makes good sense," I said. "I imagine conditions in Nigeria and Ghana are a lot like those in many other parts of Africa." Having made several trips to that continent by now and participated in eleven safaris, I at least had some idea of what to expect. Life in the larger cities like Johannesburg, Salisbury, and Nairobi was relatively easy, but the smaller towns were another matter, and all of the outlying villages were still very primitive.

"That's why, incidentally," Elder Faust continued, "the first missionary calls will be for only one year, and the first two couples who agree to serve will be encouraged to leave the country for a brief respite at about the midway point. And that's why this is not an official 'call,' not for the moment."

At that point he looked at us intently. "Ren? Rachel? We are not asking you for a definite commitment right now. We merely want you to go home and discuss the matter—ponder it—and above all talk to your Father in Heaven. Then let us know your feelings about going to West Africa and presenting the gospel formally for the very first time to members of the black race there."

For an instant Rachel and I looked at each other, *into* each other, really. I guess we were smiling, for it was one of those special moments in which words are superfluous. We were already certain of our answer. I had held many positions in the Church, never anticipating them but accepting in humility and without reservation whatever came. Furthermore, my wife had always supported me with a beautiful kind of sharing and commitment. She had been the constant night-light to my faith. In consequence, there was no reason to begin finding excuses now. "If the call should come," I replied, "we will accept. We will gladly serve wherever we are sent for as long as is necessary."

"Well," Elder Faust said thoughtfully, "we surely appreciate your spirit—but give yourself time to talk it out in private and to get down on your knees. Make absolutely certain within your hearts."

It was hardly a high-pressure sales pitch, to say the least, so cautious and conditional. Surely no one could ever go wrong in talking to the Lord, and we had done so often. Nevertheless, if our Father in Heaven, President Kimball, and the Brethren all wanted us to go, then *we* wanted to go. It was that simple, and any questions of inconvenience or hardship were irrelevant.

CHAPTER THREE

Voice of the Prophet

I t was 8:30 A.M., and I hung up the phone feeling slightly frustrated. "President Faust is not in his office," I said. "He's in the temple."

"Well," Rachel laughed, "that's not such a bad place to be."

"Granted," I replied. "It's just that now . . . well, there's our Regional Representatives seminar tomorrow, and then we're into general conference. It may be awhile before we can talk with him any further." Having discussed our prospective call and prayed about it, as instructed, we were more convinced than ever that our decision of the previous day was correct. Already we were laying plans, adjusting ourselves psychologically for the separation from our sons, Rendell Jr., Ralph, Thomas, and their wives, our daughter Jane, our grandchildren, and a multitude of beloved relatives and friends. We would be leaving behind home, recreation, my legal practice; all the old sensations that had accompanied our departure to preside over the Swiss Mission in 1965 were returning. Already I felt a poignant, growing sense of recollection. Then, however, I had been a mere youngster of fifty-seven; now I was seventy. And yet, we reminded ourselves, it would be a small sacrifice compared to those made by so many others, virtually everyone in the early days of the Church, for example. I thought of the rich young man in pursuit of salvation and the Savior's admonition, "Go and sell that thou hast, and give to the poor." (Matthew 19:21.) The young man had departed sorrowing, unable to face the challenge. Would my wife and I be able to meet the same challenge if it ever came? I hoped so. The Lord had blessed us with material abundance, but we had always sought to keep it within a spiritual perspective.

Yes, already we were undergoing a transition, and now I could hardly wait to have it made official. "Anyway," I said, "I left our phone number with Jim's secretary. Maybe he'll be calling us once he's back from the temple."

"Maybe so," Rachel replied, "but I suspect he'll be a very busy man for the next while."

Rachel was correct, more so in fact than either of us realized at the time. But our Regional Representatives seminar the following day could scarcely have offered me personally more ideal preparation for the big change in our own lives. As President Kimball arose and began to speak, I immediately felt a sense of relevance that grew with every sentence he uttered.

"Now, I repeat what I have said many times before," he told us. "We have an obligation, a duty, a divine commission to preach the gospel to every nation and to every creature." How often I had heard such exhortations from nearly all of the Brethren, yet on that particular day my whole being seemed to resonate with his message. "But, I ask you, are we advancing as fast as we should? We feel that the Spirit of the Lord is brooding over the nations to prepare the way for preaching the gospel. Certain political events have a bearing upon the spreading of the truth, and it seems as though the Lord is moving upon the affairs of men and nations to hasten their day of readiness when leaders will permit the elect among them to receive the gospel of Jesus Christ and when the gospel will be preached 'for a witness' among all nations."

President Kimball had pointed out that our fast-growing technology would be an immense boon in preaching and proselyting but added that we seemed somewhat tardy in making use of it. Despite the great advantages of rapid transportation, he said, much of the world was still untouched by the gospel.

"When we think of nations like China, the Soviet Union, India, the whole continent of Africa and our Arab brothers and sisters—hundreds of millions of our Father's children—this seems to be on my mind as I consider how big the world is now and how many people are waiting for us to move forward."

For an instant he hesitated, his countenance calm and luminous, his spirit majestic. Was it merely my imagination, or had his gaze momentarily coalesced with my own? "And what about Africa?" he demanded. "They have waited so long already. More than one-tenth of the entire population of the world is living on the African continent, nearly twice as many as the whole of South America. Are they not included in the Lord's invitation to 'teach all nations'? Are they not included in 'the uttermost parts of the earth'?"

Then, most appropriately, he read portions of a letter recently received from a schoolboy in Ghana. The young man had expressed fervent hope that he might soon be baptized a member of the Church and in time receive the priesthood. He spoke of the way his heart thrilled to the strains of "Come, Come Ye Saints," "Come, O Thou King of Kings," and other songs of Zion.

President Kimball also read excerpts from two other letters. "To testify to our faith in Ghana," one of them stated, "we have refused to yield to representatives of some churches in America who have tried to influence us with large amounts of money to cause a change of our name to theirs. We therefore solemnly declare in the name of Jesus Christ that God has prepared the groups in Ghana for you, and we have nowhere else to go but forward, looking for your missionaries to help us understand the Church better. It is our burning desire to live by that faith and attain its standards."

The third, written from Nigeria, stated, "When I read through the literature and books you sent to me there is no reason why you should not come and establish a Church here. . . . In the book Matthew 24:14 Jesus said, 'And this gospel of the kingdom shall be preached in all the world for a witness unto all nations and then shall the end come.' It is thus to be seen that nothing seemed to be as important in the sight of the Lord as to preach the kingdom of God." He then added, "If you say you cannot come and establish churches in

Nigeria, what provision have you made that the gospel of the kingdom shall be preached in all the world for a witness unto all nations? Nigeria is a country in the world . . . and if any one Church has the truth it is not only necessary that it be taught to the heathen nations . . . but also to members of other sects, for we must all come in the unity of the faith. We need salvation as you, yourself do . . . and desire that we may all come to a unity of the faith as one body."

Stirring words in every case. At the time, however, I did not realize that their authors would soon become flesh-and-blood realities, a unique and unforgettable part of my life. I did not know that all of them would enter the waters of baptism: Emmanuel Bondah, the schoolboy, and J. W. B. Johnson and Anthony Obinna, the first authorized branch presidents in Ghana and Nigeria respectively.

The next morning I attended the first session of general conference and was delighted to learn that Elder James E. Faust had been called as a member of the Council of the Twelve. Surely the past week had been a momentous one for him, but despite his ever-growing responsibilities he moved ahead with dispatch on our pending assignment to Africa. Three days later, on October 3, we met in his office, and there received another happy surprise. Ted Cannon and his wife, Janath, were to be our companions, a calling that they had not even anticipated until a few hours earlier. We were all beaming over the news, and it seemed to be an ideal combination. Not only were we friends of long standing, but the Cannons had also been called to preside over the Swiss Mission three years after our release from that position. As mentioned earlier, Ted was at this time a counselor to Elder Faust in the International Mission, and Janath had served in the general presidency of the Relief Society.

Everything was falling smoothly into place, each new event part of some grand orchestration and all of it infused with added life and meaning by the magnificent conference just concluded. It was a spiritual high that increased far more as we entered the conference room of the First Presidency and the Council of the Twelve. The prophet was seated at one end of a long, darkly gleaming table with his counselors, N. Eldon Tanner and Marion G. Romney. Other Church leaders at that meeting were Elder Faust; Elder Carlos Asay of the First Quorum of the Seventy and member of the Church Missionary Committee; Francis M. Gibbons, secretary to the First Presidency, and David Kennedy. It was, without doubt, an auspicious moment, and the next forty minutes were rich with instruction and counsel, much of it from President Kimball himself. His words were fatherly and gentle, without the slightest affectation but, as always, profound.

"We want you to know, our dear brothers and sisters," President Kimball concluded, "that this assignment will require great faith, wisdom, and courage. We appreciate you; we love and commend you for your faithfulness, and send you forth with our most fervent prayers."

How could anyone ask more? I wondered, and felt certain that same thought must have pulsed in the mind of everyone present.

"Are there any more questions?" he asked at last.

I glanced at the others. "Only one for the moment," I said. "How soon would you like us to leave?"

The prophet smiled, and his gaze was a perfect blend of mischief and benevolence. "Yesterday," he said.

Clearly, however, there was much to be done before the departure, not only to set our personal affairs in order but to assure that we as missionary representatives would be accepted in Nigeria and Ghana and that the Church itself would be legally recognized there. We left the meeting having concluded that November 1, a mere twenty-eight days hence, would be a reasonable departure date. Our official calls would arrive soon, and I had been assigned as senior companion to our little group of four.

As we left the office, Elder Carlos E. Asay made an observation none of us will ever forget. "Brothers and sisters," he said quietly, "in my opinion no missionaries in the entire history of the Church have ever received a more important and challenging call." A moving thought, but we already knew that the days ahead would bear him out.

CHAPTER FOUR

Into the Dark Continent

The jet moved on and on, scorching through the sky with a long, echoing roar. Sound and motion blended hypnotically, and it was difficult to believe that we were truly on our way. We had left the Gatwick Airport south of London at 1:00 P.M., and crossed the Channel and the entirety of France in a mere hour and a half. Below us now lay the Pyrenees. Their snowy summits projected here and there through a tattered shawl of gray clouds. Just ahead lay the eastern tip of Spain.

The whole experience was muffled in unreality now—not only the flight itself but also the entire five or six weeks preceding it: the lengthy, detailed planning and preparation for departure, reviewing letters from the files of the International Mission, the inevitable vaccinations, announcements in the press, interviewing on a local talk show, visits on my part to the embassies of Nigeria and Ghana in Washington to secure temporary visas, the numerous letters and visits from friends and relatives . . . family farewelling, replete with the usual handclasps, hugs, and kisses.

Before long we had crossed the Mediterranean Sea and were over Northern Africa. Below us, like a part of Mars, lay the vast and barren Sahara, its red sands swirling upward in storms that would ultimately die and settle over great areas of the continent. *No place for a landing,* I told myself, and before long we were moving over even darker clouds heavy with rain and occasionally flickering with lightning. Thunder from the heavens united with the constant thunder of our jet.

For a time, perhaps, we all must have felt a sense of foreboding. The day had suddenly engulfed us in a universal gloom. Despite all our planning, despite my earlier visits to Africa, we were now entering the unknown with little comprehension as to what might lie ahead. "The Dark Continent," I mused. Rachel glanced at me questioningly. I smiled and shrugged. "That's what they call it."

Some two hours later we landed at our destination: Lagos, Nigeria, there on the southern coast of midwestern Africa. Night had fallen, and we left the plane to be greeted by a surge of warm, humid air, a bit like the atmosphere Jonah must have encountered inside the whale.

The storm through which we had passed was now moving toward us, but within the airline terminal it was so hot and muggy we were soon sweating, with no chance for immediate escape. First there was a prolonged wait in the slow-moving health line, where finally our vaccination and inoculation papers were approved. Then a "line" to present our passports and entry papers, which in reality was little more than a chaotic mass of humanity, all seething about a single official. Situated upon a small stand, he simply reached out at random to accept the nearest offering. The clamor and confusion reminded me of a Chicago grain auction, and the end was not yet. Next came another seemingly interminable line where we waited to declare our financial-cash status, one of that country's monetary regulations.

Fortunately, there were plenty of men on hand willing to act as stand-ins for a fee so that we could cool ourselves periodically beneath some overhead fans. Even at that, however, it was a tedious wait, a bit like being in a mild steam bath with all our clothes on. Ted turned to me, his face beaded with perspiration but still bright with his buoyant smile. "Almost like induction into the army," he said.

I smiled back wanly. "I feel as if we're all being transformed into ground sloths."

Six months later a beautiful new airport would ease many of the woes of our first arrival, but for now other lines followed

—one to collect our baggage, and finally the wait for customs inspection. Happily, we eventually passed right on through without having to open a single bag, and all because we told them we were missionaries! Both experiences, the long and frustrated waiting as well as the respectful solicitude over our religious calling, were a distinct foretaste of things to come.

We arrived at the Federal Palace Hotel, fifteen miles away, exhausted and with only one desire—total collapse in a comfortable bed. It was 10:30 P.M. but seemed more like two in the morning.

"Reservations for two couples under the name of Mabey and Cannon," I told the desk clerk. "Our deposit was sent from Salt Lake City, Utah, some time ago."

The clerk, well dressed and businesslike, leafed through the register dubiously, squinting from time to time and frowning. At last he glanced up, his face blank. "Sir," he said sorrowfully, "I must apologize, but your reservations have been canceled. It would seem that your deposit has never arrived, and in West Africa hotel reservations must be fully paid in advance."

"But it was sent over twenty days ago," I said incredulously. The four of us stared at each other slightly dazed, both Rachel and Janath murmuring in disbelief. "Well, we'll just have to take whatever's available," I said. "We've got to have something."

The clerk shook his head, looking morose. "I'm very sorry, sir, but I'm afraid there are no rooms left."

"Oh, you must have something," Ted interjected. "We've come here all the way from the United States, and we're too tired to begin looking for other accommodations this time of night."

Eventually, after much discussion, the clerk disappeared to air our case with the management, and at last he returned smiling. The wayfarers would be taken in.

Wearily we shuffled down the hall, squishing across a stretch of carpet that, thanks to a leaky roof, was soaked with rain. Our rooms were air-conditioned, but the bathroom seemed dirty and contained no soap or towels. The tub was full of water in case the main system should be turned off during the night. One way or another, however, it appeared that water would be available for a while. The roof over the bathroom also leaked and was now welcoming the storm we had left behind. The culture shock was taking hold.

Minutes later I crumpled into bed and lay back with a groan, took a deep breath, and filled my lungs with the odor of disinfectant. "Good grief," I muttered, "what's that stench?"

"Didn't you read this little note?" Rachel inquired. " 'Dear Guest: In order to keep your room free of pests, Management has invited a pest control company to inspect it on Thursday, Nov. 9, between the hours of 9:00 A.M. and 5:00 P.M. We regret any inconvenience that this may cause. Please bear with us. General Housekeeper.' "

"Well," I said, "it may be a toss-up as to which is worse —the pests or the odor—but, ready or not, the Church has arrived in Nigeria. Tomorrow we start proselyting."

I failed to realize at the time that "tomorrow" would be a national holiday, and likewise the day after that. Then would come the Sabbath. Obviously, our first great test would fall under the heading of patience.

CHAPTER FIVE

Great Expectations

Despite our frustration over the long weekend holiday, the following two weeks were among the most eventful of our entire lives. And those events truly ran the gamut—all the way from the ludicrous and irritating to the profound and inspiring.

At the more mundane level, we rediscovered the joys of early childhood, showering in cold water, then going without showers entirely and brushing our teeth in ginger ale for want of any water whatever. We learned more about the shortage of hotel rooms, about waiting in lines (a full hour and forty-five minutes to cash a check at the local bank), about shopping for groceries that were constantly in meager supply and exorbitantly expensive. Living costs in that part of the world are extremely high, especially housing and transportation, but once we were able to lease a home and purchase a secondhand automobile we could reduce missionary costs to a manageable level.

We learned what it was like to exist in a climate that left one not only sweating but often almost wringing wet. The mere thought of a suit and tie was torture, and both Ted and I soon decided that slacks and short-sleeved white shirts were the only tolerable but still respectable missionary attire.

Although Nigeria was building its highway system as rapidly as possible, roads in general were primitive and hazardous, traffic regulations virtually nonexistent. Piles of garbage and open sewers could be found in many areas, and run-down housing intermingled with modern buildings. Postal and telephone communications were unpredictable, as were air and surface transportation, a condition that would create almost insurmountable problems for us many times in the days to come. Such trials are the natural birth pangs experienced in varying degrees by many emergent nations, and certainly the citizens and leaders of Nigeria and Ghana did their best. Never in all my travels have I discovered people who worked harder or more cheerfully.

One problem above all others, however, caused us continuing anxiety in the early days of our mission and robbed me personally of sleep more than once—that of insuring that the Church secure legal recognition. Although freedom of religion is safeguarded under the constitutions of Nigeria and Ghana, the matter of recognition was a thorny one for two basic reasons. First, there was the general disorganization and inefficiency we had encountered already. Second, a number of those self-styled "branches" of the Church, established without divine authority long before our arrival, had incorporated without Church permission or prior knowledge under the name "Church of Jesus Christ of Latter-day Saints, Inc." In consequence, the true Church could not legally use the same title without authorization from those who had already adopted it—persons who were generally unknown to us. Worse still, even if that right were granted, the result legally would be a confused mixture of the one true Church and a loose collection of other religious congregations called by the same name. Under such conditions the financial problems alone could become disastrous. Property or assets acquired by the Church, for example, might legitimately be subjected to the disposal of any organization merely bearing the same appellation, or to the creditors of that organization. This spelled endless trouble.

Simultaneously, it was imperative that we obtain the kind of official recognition that would insure our acceptance and enough stability to permit the establishment of a regular

Elder Rendell Mabey, Elder Edwin Cannon, Sister Janath Cannon, and Edet John Ikpe stand by sign of one of several unauthorized "branches" existing prior to the missionaries' arrival.

mission in West Africa. Certainly we would not be very productive missionaries sitting in prison or in exile.

In discussing the matter with two lawyers we met at the Federal Ministry of Internal Affairs, I concluded that the best procedure might be to gain control of the old corporation, then dissolve it and begin over again with new articles and filings. That too, however, was much easier said than done. The following entry from my journal, made during the first week of our arrival, probably sums up the concern as well as anything: "I wonder each day if my personal mission will not be more as a lawyer to straighten out legal entanglements—maybe placed there by the devil?"

Those were some of the negatives. Fortunately, they were greatly outweighed by the positives. And these also began manifesting themselves from the onset. More than 250 languages are still spoken in Nigeria and Ghana collectively—a

Truck sign in Accra, Ghana—typical of the country's strong, overt Christian beliefs.

condition that for obvious reasons sometimes made communication difficult. Fortunately, however, English is the official, commercial, and dominant language in those countries and is strongly encouraged by their governments. Such a condition proved a great boon, of course, in all our proselyting endeavors, including the distribution of Church literature. Without it we would have wandered in a constant babel of confusion, with no recourse but to plead for the gift of tongues.

Happily, too, in examining various book and magazine stands, we saw little of the junk literature and lurid cover photography so prevalent in many parts of the world. In their stead were publications with such titles as "Today's Story of Jesus," "In My Father's House," and "God's Chosen Fast," as well as numerous leatherbound Bibles of varying sizes in both English and the native tongues.

Billboards and vehicles of every description including motorcycles actually carried signs reading, "God Is Not Dead," "Love Thy Neighbor," "Jesus Is Coming—Are You Ready for

Him?'' "God Is My Refuge and Strength," and the exhortation, "Vote for Jesus!" A bit blatant to some minds, perhaps, but a refreshing change from the carnal and worldly enticements deluging so much of the earth these days.

At the very least, we decided, the religious atmosphere was a healthy one. Little churches dotted the landscape, and ministers of one kind or another abounded everywhere. Many times since then, in fact, I have felt that we owe a great debt to those religions which established a foothold in many parts of Africa when Christianity was regarded with much suspicion and hostility. Through their efforts a remarkably rich seedbed was prepared for sowing the everlasting gospel. Soil so fertile, in the words of an old-time farmer, it would "almost jump up and grab the seeds from your hand."

Our first actual proselyting began inadvertently, in fact, on November 11, only two days after our arrival in Lagos. That morning while posing for official missionary photos outside our hotel we met a father and son by the name of Olawayin. The older man, a village chief, lived some distance away, but his son, a resident of the city employed in an electronics business, promptly expressed his desire to know more about our work. "What is the meaning of these words, 'Latter-day Saints'?" he inquired, and I caught the knowing glances of my three companions. It was a perfect entree, and we didn't intend to lose it.

"That's a good question," I replied, "and the meaning is very important. If you have a little time in the next day or two we'd be happy to tell you about it." Already my appointment book was out, and within minutes we had arranged a meeting with Olawayin the younger at his office for 9:45 the following morning.

It was an optimistic beginning, ample compensation for any inconveniences suffered thus far, and we arrived at our appointment promptly the next morning. The office was small, with barely enough room to seat the four of us and our cab driver, a Mr. Agemuyiwa. He too had expressed an interest in our teachings and been invited to attend.

Our host had bought bottled soda water in honor of the occasion, and we reciprocated with a full-course feast of gospel doctrine, beginning with a forty-minute introduction to the

Church by Elder Cannon including illustrations from *Meet the Mormons,* by Doyle and Randall Green. Afterward, I explained the "falling away" and Latter-day Saint beliefs regarding the family and eternal marriage. Then, having noted that neither of our investigators smoked, I added a few comments about the Word of Wisdom and concluded with some observations regarding the importance of honesty and Christlike living. Finally, Rachel and Janath bore their testimonies, and our new friends both agreed enthusiastically to my suggestion that we kneel together in prayer.

It would be easy to conclude, of course, that we had "laid it on" too heavily, that it might have been far wiser to have observed the scriptural admonition about the importance of giving milk before meat. In this case, however, and in many to come, there was no way of knowing how often we might be able to meet again in the immediate future with any given person or group. Furthermore, the Spirit had been very strong that morning, and periodically throughout the presentation both investigators said they believed our words. We were striking familiar chords and they vibrated.

Afterward we explained that we would soon be moving on to southeast Nigeria, but arranged to hold another meeting at the hotel the next day. We also gave them the name and address of Elder William B. Beer, a member of the Church residing in Lagos. Brother Beer and his family were currently visiting in the United States but would be returning to Africa shortly, and during his exploratory visit in August Ted had learned that they would be happy to hold meetings.

That evening Rachel and I stood by the window of our hotel room, gazing out over the nearby harbor. Palm trees cast graceful silhouettes against the water, and the sun was an immense ball of red-gold fire sinking into the horizon. Once it had vanished, the night came swiftly, recalling my days on safari long ago. Only the lighted freighters were visible now, at anchor or moving slowly across the dark water. "Really a beautiful sight, isn't it?" my wife said.

I put my arm around her, and for a while made no reply. "Yes," I said at last, "it surely is." All those lights . . . they seemed to symbolize something. They filled us with hope and a sense of great expectation.

CHAPTER SIX

A Momentous Occasion

"Our faith is still on trial," the words read, "but with God on our side we must succeed." I had first encountered those words in a letter dated September 28, 1978, on file at the International Mission office in Salt Lake City. They had haunted me ever since. Often now I recalled other words as well—that memorable phrase, for example, read by President Kimball during our Regional Representatives meeting only a few weeks earlier: "If you say you cannot come and establish churches in Nigeria, what provision have you made that the gospel of the kingdom shall be preached in all the world for a witness unto all nations?"

Sobering, indeed, for the provision had at last been made, and we were a fundamental part of it.

The date was now November 18, 1978, only nine days after our arrival in Nigeria, and we were staying in the city of Port Harcourt. Leaving Janath behind to meet with any investigators who might call, the rest of us had set forth by taxi in search of the person who had penned those words, Mr. Anthony U. Obinna. This man was the leader of one of those congregations that had assumed the name Church of Jesus Christ of Latter-day Saints, a key figure in the history of such organizations, and he had been awaiting the day of our coming for thirteen years.

Our problem now was simply finding him. Like so many others in Nigeria, Anthony Obinna lived on a street without name or number in a village somewhere northward. The return address on his letter contained only the name of his village, county, and state—Umuelem Enyiogugu, Mbaise-Owerri, Imo State. Our driver had never heard of the place and only knew that it was somewhere near the city of Owerri, about a three-hour taxi ride from Port Harcourt.

Upon approaching Owerri, we stopped at a girls' school for directions, followed the road through a crowded native market, and were advised to continue north. At our next stop someone told us we had gone too far, but a middle-aged gentle-man with only one arm overheard our discussion and informed us that the place we sought was still three miles ahead. "I know that man Anthony Obinna," he said affably, "and the village where he lives. Let me go along and show you the way."

Our drive took us down a road flanked with heavy foliage, banana and palm trees ending in a native compound fronted by a little two-door church. Near the roof in blue letters were painted the words, "Nigerian Latter-Day Saints." Over one door were the letters "LDS," and over the other, "Missionary Home."

Under the circumstances, our arrival seemed rather mirac-ulous, and it was a curious experience encountering the name of our own church there in such humble surroundings—a remote spot halfway around the world which none of us had ever heard of until so recently, where no missionary had ever before set foot. "Well," I said, after we had stood there amazed for a moment, "let's go meet the Mormons."

The compound was filled with people—including a number of tiny children, most of whom were naked—and everyone present stared at us in astonishment. Anthony himself, how-ever, was visiting Owerri, and his son eagerly volunteered to go there with our cab driver in search of him. Forty-five minutes later he returned with a small, wiry-looking man of about thirty-five who greeted us warmly, flashing one of those white-toothed smiles so typical of his people.

"Mr. Obinna?" I said. Filled with excitement, I reached for his hand.

"Obinna, yes," he replied, "Anthony, no. I am his brother Francis." He too eyed us in wonderment, and the air seemed to be charged with electricity. Anthony, however, had been detained in Owerri for reasons that were not quite clear in the excitement of the moment.

It was a long wait in any case, during which we were introduced to other members of the Obinna family and a number of their friends. We were also invited to explore the chapel, a tiny structure with a blue door and shutters, which occupied only half of the meetinghouse. The other half of the building was a combination office and classroom. There was no glass in the windows, and nothing to cover the cement floor but a few chairs and rows of crude wooden benches. Light green walls and a white ceiling relieved the starkness, however, and the overall effect was very pleasant. We felt a good spirit.

Several of the Obinnas and their friends accompanied us. Obviously, they were proud of their facilities and hoping for a positive reaction. "This is beautiful," Rachel told them. She had just finished distributing cookies and crackers to children at the door. "So pleasant and clean." Ted and I were quick to agree.

"Notice this," Ted said quietly and gave me a nudge. On a table in front were a copy of the Doctrine and Covenants and three paperback editions of the Book of Mormon. Shelves on the wall behind contained stacks of the *Ensign* and *Church News*, and a small blackboard featured in neat lettering the program for Sunday services the following day.

During our inspection the chapel had been filling with spectators, many of them youngsters and infants. Apparently some of them had never seen a white person before, and everyone seemed to realize that something very important was happening. Our presence, in fact, had called for a spontaneous celebration. Someone had arrived with drums, musical sticks, gourds, and a large blow-jug, all of which filled our ears for the next fifteen minutes with their sound. Throughout it all, there was also much clapping and chanting—the total effect so loud, persistent, and irresistible that we had soon joined in, scarcely realizing what was happening. Looking into those faces, dark-skinned yet brimming with inner light, seeing eyes so radiant with life, absorbed in all that primitive rhythm and sound, I

Missionary and his escorts.

felt an excitement unlike anything I had ever experienced. The faces glowed, emanating emotions beyond definition. It was without doubt a momentous occasion.

Inside the "Missionary Home" a short while later we discovered a copy of *Gospel Principles,* which Ted had mailed to Anthony on October 26, already well used and stamped on the front with the words "LDS Mission," the date and location. On one wall was a picture of the Apostles of the Church, featuring Elder Boyd K. Packer as the newest member. Another wall contained a picture of our late Church President Harold B. Lee.

Throughout our visit there people, including many women and children, continued to arrive, greeting us with much curiosity and excitement. "Hello, hello—welcome, welcome, welcome . . ." According to the branch records there were seventy-one members, and it looked as though most of them were already on hand. The news of our presence had spread rapidly, but the star of this whole fascinating production had yet to arrive.

Eventually I became restless and wandered outside only to be followed by a covey of chattering children determined to escort me about the village. The man we were waiting for, who had been waiting so much longer for us, arrived shortly after my return. Solemn, gentle, and dignified, he greeted us quietly as though an overt display of enthusiasm at such a moment might be almost sacrilegious. Our eyes, however, were moist. We all felt movingly the richness of God's Spirit.

CHAPTER SEVEN

Meeting Obinna

$\mathcal{M}$inutes after that first memorable encounter, we had gathered together again in the Missionary Home, and there Anthony Uzodimma Obinna gave us the details of his background. An assistant to the local head schoolmaster, he was forty-eight years old and had been longing and praying for the missionaries ever since November 1965.

"It has been a long, difficult wait," he said, "but that doesn't matter now. You have come at last."

"A long wait, yes," Ted agreed, "and I guess it's hard for all of us to remember that man's time is not God's time, especially when we want something so desperately . . . but the gospel is really here now in all its fulness."

Our new investigator nodded reflectively. Like a man rescued after years in the wilderness, he seemed to be filled with awe and incredulity. Perhaps it was a bit difficult for all of us to comprehend the significance of what was happening and what lay ahead. In the meantime, we were becoming acquainted.

The name "Uzodimma," Anthony explained, was bestowed upon him by his parents and meant "the best way," whereas "Obinna" meant "one who is very dear to his father." Certainly the face with its large, rather wide-set eyes, its long, solemn upper lip, and sensitive, expressive mouth seemed appropriate to the names. The names, in turn, seemed appropriate to the man. Anthony Obinna definitely emanated a spirituality that imparted warmth and trust.

"In the year 1965," he related, "I was visited in my dreams by a tall and majestic man who carried a walking stick in his right hand. He asked me whether I had ever read about Christian and Christiana from Bunyan's *A Pilgrim's Progress.* I replied that I had but that it was long ago and that I had forgotten much of the story. I was then told to read it again—which I later did."

Pausing, he regarded us serenely, and I felt the kind of anticipation that comes when someone is about to offer a priceless possession for inspection.

"After several months," he continued, "that same personage appeared in another dream, and this time he took me to a beautiful building and showed me everything inside. Later, he returned one final time. Then came the Nigerian civil war, and one day while confined to the house for safety, I began to read an old copy of the *Reader's Digest* and discovered an article entitled 'The March of the Mormons.' I had never even heard of the word 'Mormon,' but there before my eyes—" he hesitated, getting a firm grip on his emotions—"was the very building I had visited in my dream."

From the time he had finished that magazine article his mind had never rested. Immediately he had rushed out to tell his brothers the news and later, upon written request, received a copy of the Book of Mormon along with "Joseph Smith's Testimony" and other pamphlets from Salt Lake City. Later still, he met a member of the Church, Lamar Williams, who was in Africa on business. Brother Williams explained important aspects of the gospel and afterward sent him additional Church literature.

Having discovered that there were no immediate plans to organize the Church in Nigeria, Anthony became deeply depressed. He refused to abandon hope, however, and continued to write letters to Salt Lake City requesting that the gospel be brought to his people. Despite persecution and abuse from members of his community, he continued to pray and study. He dreamed often of the missionaries, never forsaking his faith in Jesus Christ or the conviction that the gospel would one day arrive in all its fulness. Meanwhile, he united with his brothers and family in teaching their new religious beliefs to others. If the Church could not be established in Black Africa, he at least wanted to live by and share its precepts as closely as possible and to adopt its name.

It was a long and inspiring story, but that was not the end of our discussion. Having asked my companions to remain and teach the gospel to the others present, I accompanied Anthony to the adjoining room for a private interview. There we discussed Nigerian law and whether it might contain any restrictions that would prevent us from performing baptisms. Despite the problems of incorporation mentioned earlier, however—the fact that we were not yet an officially recognized religion there—Anthony assured me that we would have no problems. "Well," I said, feeling relieved, "I'm delighted to hear that. We must do a lot of traveling during the next few weeks to visit other groups like your own. We have the names and general locations but don't know much about their present status. Consequently, it may be about six weeks before we can return to hold a baptism, but in the meantime you would have a good opportunity to prepare your people more fully for membership in the true Church."

Anthony Obinna, however, did not look happy. "No, please," he said quietly, "I know that there are many others, but we have been waiting for thirteen years." His eyes were filled with longing. "Please, if it is humanly possible—go ahead with the baptisms now!"

For a few seconds we merely sat there looking into each other's eyes. "Are most of your people truly ready?" I asked at last.

Anthony nodded emphatically. "Yes—absolutely, yes! They know, as I do, that the gospel has been restored, but we must have guidance and direction. Let us baptize those strongest in the faith now and teach the others further."

The Spirit was very strong, the man's goodness and testimony clearly evident. "In that case," I said, "we will conduct the baptism as soon as possible." Pausing, I consulted my appointment book. "We have commitments tomorrow and the next day which must be honored, but Tuesday the twenty-first, three days from now, is open. Would that be satisfactory?"

"Oh, yes, indeed!" he exclaimed. "Wonderful!"

"You realize, of course," I continued, "that every candidate for baptism must be interviewed beforehand just as you have been—to insure worthiness and the existence of a living testimony. Every person, young or old, must be convinced that the gospel has been restored through the Prophet Joseph Smith. They must be convinced that The Church of Jesus Christ of Latter-day Saints is the only true church upon the earth, that it is built upon a foundation of living Apostles and prophets who are continually guided by revelation from on high. They must know that President Spencer W. Kimball is a prophet, seer, and revelator who speaks the mind and will of God. They must also be willing to live all the commandments faithfully and understand that the gospel is a complete way of life sometimes demanding great sacrifice. It is not merely a Sunday religion, or a religion of convenience."

"Yes, yes, certainly," came the reply. "These are the very things that attracted us to begin with."

Before returning to Port Harcourt that evening, I also interviewed Anthony's wife, Fidelia. Because Fidelia spoke no English, her husband interpreted, but it soon became apparent that she too had a powerful testimony. "Your wife is a fine woman," I remarked in conclusion. "She has a beautiful spirit."

Anthony interpreted my message, and they both looked very pleased. "Yes, she is," he agreed. "God has blessed me greatly with a good and loving woman. When I smile she smiles; when I cry she cries."

Afterward we discussed potential baptismal sites. During my safari days I had learned to respect the waters of Africa, knowing that within the depths of some lurked creatures and diseases fatal to man. Consequently, I felt a need to inspect any proposed baptismal water personally, but Anthony assured us that there would be no problem. He had already selected a beautiful spot near the village Amakayohia on a river some four miles distant, and knew that it was safe.

"And no crocodiles?" Ted inquired, perhaps only half joking.

Our friend smiled and shook his head. "No crocodiles, I assure you—only an occasional fish."

CHAPTER EIGHT

The First Baptism

The following day was the Sabbath, and we began our morning with a banana and a piece of cheese. A meager breakfast, true, but it was the best we could manage given the availability of appetizing food and the demanding schedule ahead. By nine o'clock we had traveled a short distance to attend a meeting with a young man named Gilbert Onyiri at his family compound on Gambia Street in Diobu, a suburb of Port Harcourt.

Gilbert had recently been converted to the Church and ordained a priest while studying in Switzerland. Shortly thereafter he had returned to his African home with the "good news" and a burning testimony. As far as we knew, in fact, he was the only black priesthood bearer in all of Africa at the time.

Eleven young men and women were present at that meeting. All were Gilbert's family members or friends, and he was eager for them to learn more about the gospel. His enthusiasm was not misplaced by any means. At the end of our presentation several requested Church membership, and we agreed to hold a baptism six weeks hence, having arranged for them to study regularly with Brother Onyiri in the meantime.

Afterward we journeyed to his home village of Ogbogu, an hour and a half by taxi to the north. Gilbert had also arranged this meeting in order to have us teach the gospel to his parents and neighbors, and we convened in a tiny church building crammed with investigators. People were hunched together in the aisles and little entrance hall; others clustered about outside and peered in through the grilled windows. As nearly as I could determine, about ninety villagers were on hand to hear our message.

During the hour that followed, Brother Onyiri interpreted, concluding with a powerful testimony of his own. The village chief then arose to affirm everything that had been said. "What these people have told us today is true," he announced, "and I therefore wish to provide land upon which to construct a new church. It is very clear that we need more room—far more room—because many people will be joining this religion very soon."

Ted and I exchanged glances, shaking our heads a bit in amazement. *Can this really and truly be happening?* I wondered. The whole thing seemed incredible. Did such people actually comprehend what we were offering, or were they merely caught up in the spirit of the group, momentarily captivated by something extraordinary? Would they not respond with equal enthusiasm to any new and colorful religion that might present itself? How would we fare compared to some flamboyant huckster who really "played to the gallery" with plenty of hallelujahs and praise-the-Lords? Certainly many of our investigators appeared to have that kind of orientation. Such misgivings gradually dissipated, however, giving way to the conviction that those people had truly found the only religion they desired.

Drenched with sweat but filled with rejoicing, promising to return in a few weeks for a baptism, we left the little meetinghouse. Meanwhile they too would study under the guidance of Brother Gilbert Onyiri in preparation. "All these people are very, very poor," I wrote in my journal that night, "and the conditions under which they live are unbelievable—yet they are children of God, and I feel their trust in us as the way to salvation. We must not fail them. We will not."

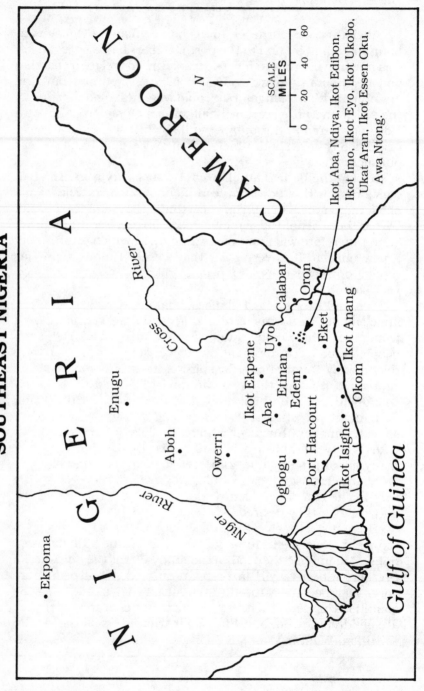

SOUTHEAST NIGERIA

Ikot Aba, Ndiya, Ikot Edibon,
Ikot Imo, Ikot Eyo, Ikot Ukobo,
Ukat Aran, Ikot Essen Oku,
Awa Ntong.

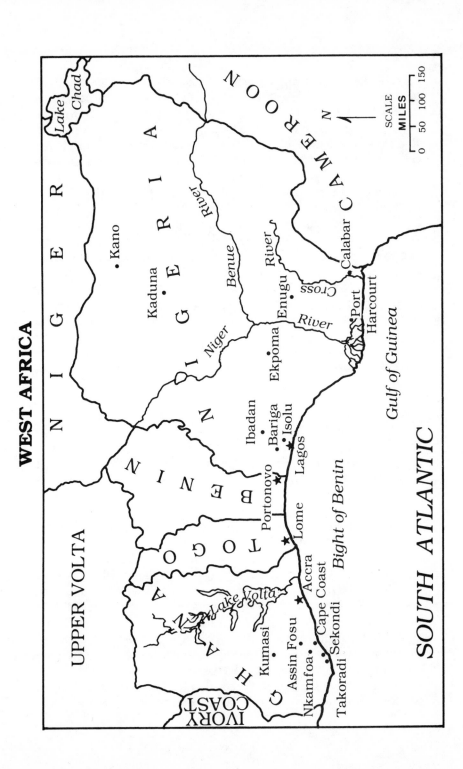

WEST AFRICA

The next morning we left Port Harcourt, traveling about 250 miles by air to Enugu, capital of Nigeria's Anambra State. There we met with two white member families from Utah—the A. Bruce Knudsens and David N. Bowns. Brothers Knudsen and Bown held doctoral degrees in biology and were employed by the United Nations World Health Organization to help combat malaria, a disease that takes one million human lives each year. Both families were outstanding Latter-day Saints, becoming a source of great aid and comfort from the onset.

At the advice of Brother Bown, we decided to hold our baptismal service with Anthony Obinna and his people as early the following day as possible. That way, we hoped, we could return to Enugu before dark and thus minimize the very real danger of robbery, even threat to life itself. Rather recently Nigeria had experienced a tragic civil war between the north and the south, which the south had lost. Many of the surrendering soldiers, however, had hidden their weapons in the forests and were now using them to relieve unwary travelers of all they possessed, automobiles included. The area surrounding our destination, in fact, was said to be one of the most dangerous in Nigeria.

Our first day in Enugu was filled with planning, and in anticipation of the great record-keeping demands to come, I asked Sister Janath Russell Cannon to serve as mission clerk. Sister Cannon accepted without hesitation, was promptly set apart, and fulfilled her calling with great dedication and efficiency from that time forward.

A cock was crowing just before daylight the following morning, and we arose early, full of excitement. November 21, 1978: Although the events of that day may never be recorded for the world at large, it was to become a great landmark in the history of the Church and among the peoples of Black Africa.

We left Enugu with the Knudsens and Bowns in the Knudsen family bus at 7:30 A.M., expecting to arrive at our destination, Umuelem Enyiogugu, by 9:00 A.M. This time, though, we were approaching the village from an opposite direction and again experienced problems finding our way over difficult roads. As a result, we arrived an hour and a half late to find the villagers both elated and anxious. They were all waiting and had sent a truck out in search of us. Several local officials had even been on hand as a welcoming committee but had eventually returned to their work a few miles away.

Our first order of business, therefore, was to visit those men in their offices. There we offered apologies for arriving late, extended greetings from President Kimball and the Council of the Twelve, and were treated much like visiting royalty. "We have heard very good things about your religion," the commissioner informed us, "and we want you to know that you are welcome. Our area government will be happy to assist you in becoming established here." He went on to praise Anthony Obinna as an outstanding member of the community, and again we were filled with wonderment. How often on missions to other countries we had felt maligned and rejected, or at best merely tolerated! How long and how hard we had scraped and struggled to find a single open-minded listener. And now this—actual assistance from the government itself! Was it only a dream after all?

No—no dream. Only a short while later we were back at the village discussing Church procedures and interviewing the nineteen adults whose names Anthony had provided. Many others desired baptism, he explained, but these were the strong ones, our foundation stones.

Meanwhile, Sister Knudsen had been teaching a number of women and children one of the Church's all-time musical favorites, "I Am a Child of God." Her listeners learned quickly and within short order were marching together throughout the village compound singing the words with great enthusiasm and harmony. "I am a child of God, and he has sent me here, has given me an earthly home with parents kind and dear." How does one describe the depth of emotion at hearing those voices? They rose spontaneously and rapturously among the trees and rooftops of that little village. "Lead me, guide me, walk beside me, help me find the way. Teach me all that I must do to live with him someday."

Yes, we all had tears in our eyes, but events were happening so rapidly and unexpectedly it was difficult to assimilate them. We merely knew that the Lord's hand was increasingly evident that day, at every turn. Even before the singing had ended, our friend Anthony informed us that fifteen leaders, village chiefs and others from the surrounding area, had arrived and wished to confer with me. I therefore excused myself and went to meet them, leaving the interviewing to Elders Cannon, Knudsen, and Bown.

All of these visitors were representatives of the Ibo Tribe, one of the largest and most influential in the country. Despite Nigeria's rapid evolution toward democracy and the establishment of government at local, state, and national levels, tribes like the Ibo, which consisted of several million people, still have much influence. These larger tribes, in fact, make the unification of Nigeria difficult in some ways because people there still tend to vote for their own tribesmen during elections.

Our meeting was held in the "Missionary Home," and it was another experience that will never be erased: fifteen leaders of influence, appearing from nowhere, it seemed, all very dark, handsome, and dignified, several wearing brilliant native robes of red, orange, blue, green, purple, and gold, all sitting there attentively while I explained the everlasting gospel. Most of them did not speak English, so Anthony interpreted, and it soon became evident that he was doing an excellent job. "Will it be possible," one of the men inquired, "to obtain a larger meetinghouse in a more central location? It may be that many of our people will become members of your church, and in that event the accommodations here would be inadequate."

In reply I explained that such a thing might be possible, that it would, of course, depend upon growth in membership. I also told them that the Church might offer financial assistance in such an undertaking but only after the members had displayed a strong desire to help themselves. Not long afterward, incidentally, the Obinna family donated a large building site to the Church. The land was located about a mile away so that other villagers would not feel they were attending the "Obinna Family Church," a point the owners emphasized in offering such a gift.

"Will your church be willing to establish schools in this area?" another man inquired.

"That I can't say," I answered. "Such considerations must await the future." I paused, listening to our interpreter, then

Aboh Branch building site, where construction has since been completed.

added, "I must tell you in all honesty, however, that The Church of Jesus Christ of Latter-day Saints does not come with material incentives and worldly goods. We come instead with a gift that can never be equaled, one worth more than all the oil in Nigeria. We come with the gift of eternal life."

For a moment there was some rather animated discussion among the men—hands gesturing, faces earnest and intelligent, highly expressive. Then I turned to Anthony Obinna, fearing that our listeners had been harboring false expectations. "What are they saying?" I asked guardedly.

"They say," he replied, and smiled faintly, watching me from the corners of his eyes, "that they wish to be baptized on your next visit."

The day, in terms of richness and fulfillment, might easily have ended right there, but the high point was yet ahead, four miles away on the Ekeonumiri River. It was there only an hour later that our first baptismal service took place. The spot selected lay at the end of a narrow dirt road amid lush greenery and palm trees, a scene that could perhaps rival the Garden of Eden. The river was rather small, only thirty or forty feet wide and so shallow that complete immersion appeared unlikely at first. After a little exploration, however, we discovered an ideal spot as one of the men in our group hacked a sizable opening among the water reeds with his machete.

Four white wrap-arounds had been acquired for the occasion which could be quickly transferred from one person to the next, and the service began promptly with an invocation by Brother Bown and a talk on the purpose of baptism by Brother Knudsen. The time had now arrived, and I entered the river with an immense sensation of incredulity and reverence, feeling its cool, gentle flow against my legs and the squishing of soft, wet sand between my toes. Reaching out for the man behind me, I took him by the hand. We smiled at each other, and I placed a hand upon his shoulder to steady us. Then, reaching across his chest with my left arm, I took him by the wrist, placing his opposite hand upon my own wrist.

For a moment we glanced at each other again—the blue eyes and the brown. Fanning out and away from us lay the river, copper colored along its fringes, swirling and green further on, and dappled with rays of sunlight. Beyond lay the vastness of Africa, and above, the endless depths of azure sky. Tiny, brightly colored fish darted to and fro in the shallows, and the onlookers there on shore waited in profound silence. We were all in the midst of a dream.

I raised my right arm to the square. "Anthony Uzodimma Obinna . . ." Bowing my head slightly, I could see the white hand clasping the black wrist, the black hand clasping the white wrist, pulse beat to pulse beat. Never had I witnessed a more complete symbol of love and brotherhood, of complete unity. It was as though the blood in our veins had blended. The sunlight reflected brilliantly from his dark brow and cheekbones. "Having been commissioned of Jesus Christ, I baptize you in the name of the Father, and of the Son, and of the Holy Ghost. Amen."

Then he descended beneath the water in that special symbol of burial and resurrection, of planting and germination, of cleansing and purification, which only complete immersion can ever satisfy. He descended into the depths and came up dripping and radiant, just as the Savior himself once did so long ago in the Jordan; and from the onlookers thronging the shore arose an audible sigh, the laughter of joy and relief springing from a great and overwhelming sense of awe and fulfillment.

The moment had come. Brother Anthony Obinna's thirteen years of waiting were over, and the first baptism of our mission had been performed. The doors of the gospel had opened upon the Dark Continent, and the light was pouring forth.

A Branch Takes Life

Lagos, Nigeria
December 4, 1978

President James E. Faust
International Mission
47 East South Temple
Salt Lake City, Utah
84150, USA

Dear President Faust:

W e have just completed a survey of that portion of
Nigeria that was indicated to be currently the most
fertile for Church purposes, as based on the files of the
International Mission and the Legal Department, the on-
site investigation of Elders Bateman and Cannon in
August, 1978, and our own observations. We report as
follows:

1. Headquarters
   It is felt that the most centrally located principal city in,
or adjacent to, a current likely productive area is Enugu, in

the Anambra State of Nigeria. Enugu is the capital city of the state, a typical Nigerian large city, sprawling over a big acreage and with no easily definable center. While Enugu does not support an international airport, the air schedules are several daily, with good equipment making 50-minute flights to the international airport in Lagos. The city also ties in well with air transportation to all parts of Nigeria.

Nigeria is in the process of constructing some very good highways, spottily located, with completion dates a year or more away. One such highway is approaching Enugu. Most other roads are dirt or poorly maintained hard-surface, containing not only chuckholes but real "booby traps." Nevertheless, Enugu is only two or three hours away by automobile from most of the working areas we have selected.

Communication in Nigeria by mail, telephone, telex, or telegraph is in dire need of betterment. Enugu is no exception, but also no worse; Lagos might be a little better, but even there, such service is unpredictable, undependable, and uncertain. Service might be completed in several minutes, several hours, several days, or never. For this reason, President Faust, we request your private telephone number, promising not to get you out of bed (eight-hour time lag) too often.

Housing is very tight, expensive, and difficult to obtain. Sometimes occupancy is delayed for a period of a year or more. With the help of friends and the Lord we have now located a headquarters place consisting of one wing of a duplex house situated at Ekulu West, Plat 30 A, Enugu.

Thus began the second of my many official reports to the Church written during our year-long mission in Africa. The accommodations were indeed expensive. The entire yard was surrounded by a chain-link fence and under the surveillance of a night watchman armed with a bow and arrow and a whistle because of frequent burglaries in the area.

Obtaining and preparing proper food was another challenge. Often Rachel and Janath journeyed to store after store to keep us supplied with groceries. A jar of peanut butter here, if one were quick on the uptake, a package of powdered sugar (usually hardened and lumpy) there, a sack of flour elsewhere. Often the latter contained weevils and, in some cases, worms. Fresh fruit and vegetables had to be disinfected with a preparation called Milton, each bottle of which bore a label promising that "the contents of this container will kill any known germ." A comforting thought, but at times we wondered whether a substance that lethal could distinguish fully between human beings and bacteria. As a further precaution against the ravages of microorganisms, we purchased imported meat in tins or cans—occasional small hams, for example, or meatball stew. Such items were slightly staggering in price, but so was practically everything.

Despite all, it was a great relief to have a home and headquarters after dwelling in shabby hotel rooms at seventy-five dollars and more a night. The place was well furnished right down to the dishes, kitchen utensils, and bed linen. (A Danish family had had to return home in an emergency, and their company sold it to us "as is.") It was also gratifying to know that we had settled upon a base of operations and to feel that our decision was the sound result of much discussion and prayer. Our new residence gave us a feeling of security and stability, a sense of direction that had steadily become more urgent.

In preparing reports for Elder Faust back home, I reflected frequently upon all that had happened within our first three weeks—enough, literally, to fill three years in an average existence.

Following his baptism, Anthony Obinna had been confirmed a member of the Church by Elder Cannon. Elder Cannon then baptized Anthony's brother Francis, the remaining baptisms and confirmations being performed with the assistance of Elders Knudsen and Bown. Then, back at the little chapel, Anthony, Francis, and their brother Raymond were ordained priests and set apart as president, first counselor, and second counselor respectively over the first divinely authorized branch of the Church in Black Africa.

Sister Fidelia Obinna was sustained as Relief Society president and set apart by her husband, thus becoming the first black woman on the African continent to hold that position. In conclusion, we created the Imo State District,

Candidates line up during the first baptismal service.

Elders Cannon and Mabey with Aboh Branch presidency, Obinna brothers (l. to r.) Raymond (second counselor), Anthony (president), and Francis (first counselor). At right is Imo State District President Bruce Knudsen.

Elder Rendell Mabey baptizes Evarist Obinna of Aboh on day of the first baptisms.

having set Elder Bruce Knudsen apart as president with special instructions to keep a watchful eye on the new Aboh Branch. The branch had been named after the area from which most of its members would probably originate.

We had arrived back in Enugu about 8:00 P.M., and four hours later I was still up, writing in my journal, exhausted and bleary eyed, but very, very happy. "It is now midnight," I concluded. "Tired, yes, but what a glorious day!"

Two days afterward in Calabar, a seaport some two hundred miles southeast of Enugu, we had managed to search out an investigator named E. Daniel Ukwat, the man who directed us to our first encounter with the Evangelist Bassey J. Ekong and his congregation in the village of Isighe, as recorded in the first chapter of this book. As mentioned, it had been an inspiring encounter, coming as it did after twenty-four hours of fasting and prayer on the part of those people that God would send them missionaries bearing the everlasting gospel.

Before leaving Isighe we had promised to meet with B. J. Ekong and his congregation at their planned conference, one they agreed to reschedule for the last three days of December for our convenience.

Later that evening back in Calabar we also met with a Brother Ime Eduok who offered to furnish transportation on the following day and direct us to other churches like the one at Isighe. One of seven bona fide Church members in the area, Ime had been baptized along with his wife in 1971 while attending school in Los Angeles, California, and had returned to Africa without receiving the priesthood. At one time he had acted as chairman of the administrative committee over all those self-styled "LDS Churches" within the Cross River area. The committee's main objective had been to unify them under the same leadership, and some progress had been made.

In addition, as an officer of the Cross River Lines (operators of ferry boats), he had proven to be a valuable source of information regarding conditions in that general locale, legal and otherwise. Even though the true Church had not been available to him upon his return to Nigeria, he had remained faithful, and we concluded our meeting with him convinced that he should receive the priesthood and that a branch should be organized in Calabar.

First Relief Society organized in Black Africa, that of Aboh Branch. The president, Fidelia Obinna, is fourth from left in back row.

In writing my mission reports I was reminded of how the days hurtled by, and scenes from the recent past were constantly running through my mind: the hazardous driving conditions and a dead cyclist by the roadside . . . newspaper reports of ritual murders performed by juju priests and accounts of witchcraft . . . children grinning wherever we went and calling, 'oyibo, oyibo'' (white man, white man) . . . the red dust constantly sifting in on hot wind—the harmattan—from the great Sahara thousands of miles northward . . . plans to purchase a '73 Volkswagen from the Bowns . . . our growing love and friendship with our missionary companions, Ted and Janath. . . . Surely we could not have asked for a finer association. Ten years my junior, Elder Cannon was a constant source of energy, ever ready to hail taxis, negotiate with drivers, stand in long lines at the airport—always moving forward tirelessly in the work, his mind teeming with information and pertinent details. Our wives also were a source of endless strength to us, truly dedicated missionaries who often bolstered each other's morale in time of need.

On December 5 we left Enugu, Nigeria, and the newly acquired home which would soon be ready for occupancy, to make our first trip to the country of Ghana. After long and tedious waiting at the airport in Lagos, we were finally on our way in a flight that would take us four hundred miles westward along the coastline and across the nations of Dahomey and Togo to our destination. We landed at Accra, Ghana's capital city, a short time later.

Thus, within slightly less than a month, the gospel had now entered a second country in Black Africa, and shortly after our arrival we had made our first contact—with a member of the Church named Lowell E. Diamond. A procurement officer for the United States Embassy, he had lived for some time in Accra with his wife, Shirley, and their twin children. That night we also met John and Louisa Waby, a young couple from England who had recently been baptized. John now worked for a large petroleum company in Ghana as a resident engineer, and both families soon became a valuable support to us. If I ever receive a mansion on high, I do not believe I will appreciate it more than I did the homes of those two good families which were opened to us so generously and so often.

Brother Diamond visited our hotel at noon on the very day of our arrival bearing a bottle of cold boiled water, a gift we truly appreciated. In Ghana and Nigeria the water supply was always uncertain. Often a twist of the tap brought nothing but a faint exhalation of trapped air, and even when water was available it had to be purified through boiling and filtering, or other means, before one dared drink it. Later at our home in Enugu, in fact, we once went thirty-one straight days without a drop of tap water in the home.

We spent much of that first afternoon in a taxi searching for another Church member named John Augustus Osei, a lawyer and native of Ghana who had taken leave of his temporary teaching position at Brigham Young University to assist us in obtaining legal recognition. Although our initial search was fruitless, we did unearth some valuable information at the Land Registry Office the next morning. There we eventually located a file labeled, "The Church of Jesus Christ of Latter-day Saints (Mormon Church) Ghana Mission," and dated July 26, 1969. Related information stated that the Church headquarters were in Utah and listed the names of five local trustees appointed at a so-called Elders' meeting on April 23 of the

Missionaries with the Reverend A. Frank Mensah outside the school in Accra where he taught.

Clement Osekre and his son with missionaries.

same year, all without knowledge or sanction from Salt Lake City.

Unfortunately, the constitution detailing the rights and functions of that organization was rather confusing and also inconsistent with official Church policy in various ways. Again, therefore, we faced the basic problem that we had encountered in Nigeria, and for that reason we desired to meet as soon as possible with the trustees. In the process, we hoped that they would be responsive to our suggestions, willing to dissolve the old corporation and establish a new one under the umbrella of the true Church. If not, we would have to follow some other procedure.

Fortunately, Ted and I were able to meet with one of the five trustees, the Reverend Dr. A. Frank Mensah, the following day. A prime leader in filing the original articles of incorporation, the Reverend Mensah proved highly cooperative and readily agreed to make the changes recommended. He also introduced us to Clement Osekre, another trustee, and both men indicated a strong desire to learn more about the gospel. They agreed as well to accompany us to Cape Coast to meet a third trustee, the Reverend J. W. B. (Joseph William Billy) Johnson.

We returned to our hotel tired, perspiring, and happy to find that the Lord had again blessed our efforts. There in the lobby was John A. Osei, who had arrived in Ghana from the United States several days earlier. Handsome, smiling, and cheerful, he listened attentively to all that had transpired and agreed that our proposals were sound. The next day he met with us in Cape Coast, about ninety miles to the southwest, helping me draft the new articles of incorporation and introducing us to investigators there.

"All day long I have felt the Spirit of the Lord very strongly," I wrote afterward, "and tonight everything seems 'in place.' I feel that the next ten days will be historical ones for the Church in Ghana."

CHAPTER TEN

Onward to Ghana

We arrived in Cape Coast on a crowded government bus to be met by Brother Osei and our corporation trustees Frank Mensah, Clement Osekre, and J.W.B. Johnson. Though his name gave no clue, Mr. Johnson was black, a citizen of Ghana, and—to our pleasure and surprise—the leader of ten different congregations in that area. In the days to follow we came to know him as a humble, spiritual man and a fine leader.

All of those congregations had adopted the title Church of Jesus Christ of Latter-day Saints, and that evening we convened with one of the largest groups yet at their church building in Cape Coast. More than a hundred people were present for a meeting that began, appropriately enough, with the congregation singing "Come, Come Ye Saints." There were crucifixes on the walls, along with several paintings of Joseph Smith praying, and toward the front a white statue of what appeared to be the Angel Moroni, a trumpet raised to his lips. Palm leaves decorated the windows and other parts of the building.

Following the singing, we were introduced by the Reverend Johnson amid much enthusiastic clapping, and each of us spoke on a basic aspect of the gospel. At the conclusion, a good

58

many of those present thronged about requesting baptism, and after Elder Cannon and I had interviewed thirty-four people, we departed for the night, promising to continue the next morning.

The first cock crowed at 4:30 A.M. the following day, and the light began to come amid the chirps and warbling of countless birds. We had stayed in quarters at the University of Cape Coast the preceding night, and now, strolling the campus alone at dawn, I found myself enthralled by the sounds and exotic odors. On every side, the walkways and grounds abounded with shrubbery and flowers of many varieties—brilliant reds and yellows, creams and golds. As usual, the sun rose explosively in a great ruddy ball the color of molten slag.

It was one of those glorious mornings when the very cells seem to scintillate in perfect unison with their surroundings and the promise of things to come. In talking with the Reverend Johnson a short while later, in fact, I learned that all of the other nine branches contained people of strong testimony much like those of Cape Coast. "They too are waiting," he explained, "and many of them are equally prepared to receive the gospel." He regarded me appraisingly. "In all honesty, I feel certain that you can baptize a thousand or more the moment you are available."

As he spoke those words I began to tingle. How many missionaries in the history of this world ever received encouragement of that kind! Simultaneously, I had to face the demands of practicality. "That's a marvelous thought," I told him, "but we must be cautious about proceeding too rapidly. We must take pains to organize thoroughly and to make certain that each branch is established on a firm foundation with capable leadership and with members who are strong in their acceptance of Joseph Smith's testimony. Otherwise, our efforts may actually do more harm than good in the long run."

Our new friend nodded solemnly. "I'm sure that you are correct," he said. "That is definitely the path we must follow."

There was one other matter, however, which gave me pause, and I selected my words carefully. "I'm told that you are a paid minister," I continued, "that you receive a livelihood through donations from your members." He nodded again. "And, of course," I added, "that is how most religions function. It is an honorable way of making a living. Within the true Church of Jesus Christ, however, we have no paid ministry. Are you aware of that fact?"

"Yes," came the reply, "I am."

"Then you also understand that Church leaders must often put in many hours each week and at times make great sacrifice. How will you survive if the Lord calls you to such a position?"

My friend smiled, slowly lifting his gaze toward the sky. "I have been thinking about that," he said, "and am sure the Lord will not call me without providing a way. As a matter of fact, my brother and I plan to acquire a farm to raise fruit, vegetables, and chickens. He is willing to provide the financial backing, and we hope to develop a model kind of farming program which others may follow. We intend, in fact, to give all our surplus to the Church."

I made no reply for some time. It was hard to restrain the tears.

At ten o'clock, having left Elder Cannon to complete the interviewing, I set forth with the Reverend Johnson along the ocean in search of a baptismal site. At one point we found the beach crowded with people pulling in an immense fish net that appeared to be nearly half a mile long, and I thought of how the Savior had once likened the kingdom of heaven "unto a net, that was cast into the sea, and gathered of every kind" (Matthew 13:47). A short distance beyond, we discovered a secluded and tranquil spot behind a barrier of rocks, but wondered whether it might become too deep and turbulent with the rising afternoon tide. Further still, we inspected the water in a small lagoon even though it was rather brackish. At our request, a fisherman in search of crabs tested the depth with his shovel and found it to be about waist level—almost ideal. The bottom, however, was encrusted with sharp-edged shells that cut his feet. In consequence, we elected to baptize at our first inspection site behind the rocks, hoping that the tide would cooperate.

We decided to hold our preliminary service in the church meetinghouse, knowing that the beach would be scorching by afternoon. The building was a large one for that area, about eighty by one hundred feet, and was being rented for two hundred cedis (about eighty dollars in U.S. currency) a year. In anticipation of our arrival, however, members of the congregation had raised 5,858 cedis for a building fund within only one month. Aware that soaring inflation would devaluate currency in Ghana by approximately 50 percent within the coming year, they planned to spend this money promptly for cement to construct their own building blocks. A number of non-members were also contributing, and it was hoped that 10,000 cedis could be raised over the next two months.

Certainly, these people had manifested the attitude of self-help to which I had referred in our meeting with the village leaders in Nigeria two weeks or so earlier. Nearly everyone we had encountered seemed to vibrate with faith and the spirit of sacrifice. Our teaching and testimonies found a receptive audience, and the interviews that followed were most encouraging. It was a fine atmosphere in which to conduct a baptism.

By 4:00 P.M. we had gathered at the beach. Behind us rose a dark green hillside, before us the emerald water, breaking in gentle frills of white along the shoreline. Eighty-nine prospective members—men, women, and children—were assembled, all clad in white, awaiting their rendezvous with eternity.

Elder Cannon entered the water first, extending his hand to Abraham Frank Mensah, and thus occurred the first divinely authorized baptism of one of God's black children in all of Ghana. Brother Mensah arose from the ocean glowing, the water dripping and shimmering from his dark hair and beard —and for a moment, despite the marked difference in skin color, Elder Cannon and our new convert looked very much alike in their brotherhood and rejoicing. It was an appropriate "first" because Frank Mensah had very possibly been the first man to organize a so-called LDS Church in the land of Ghana.

Throughout that entire afternoon the baptisms continued, Elder Cannon and I alternating one after another, the water dancing with light like millions of diamonds. Those first baptized also acted as witnesses, and Janath and Rachel carefully recorded all the necessary information.

Afterward, still in our wet clothing, we placed a chair upon the sand, and I confirmed Brother Frank Mensah, initiating an undertaking that would continue well into the night. The sun vanished and darkness settled, but the moon soon rose, three-quarters full, pale and luminous like quicksilver, casting shadows upon the sand. Meanwhile, the sacred ordinances continued, the laying on of hands, the sense of life and energy pulsing beneath. ". . . and confirm you a member of The Church of Jesus Christ of Latter-day Saints, and say unto you, receive the Holy Ghost."

And there, at our very feet, was the growing voice of the sea. It came and ebbed, came and ebbed, wave after wave, in a universal affirmation.

CHAPTER ELEVEN

Reflections at Christmas

Dec. 25, 1978

This is the first Christmas since Rachel and I have known each other that we did not exchange gifts. Just being together in the Lord's work is gift enough.

The memory of last evening lingers: A delicious dinner at the Knudsens' and afterward, the children with the aid of their father's slide projector re-enacted the story of Joseph and Mary—using towels and bathrobes for costumes, and two live goats for a background. Each of the adults present also participated. Ted and Janath sang a duet, "Holy Night," in German, Janath playing the accompaniment on the zither.

Afterward, Rachel really surprised me, and everyone else, by reciting from memory with great warmth and feeling, "The Night Before Christmas." She did it without hesitation or the slightest hitch and later explained that she had memorized it as a little girl and retained the whole thing ever since.

I read a Christmas story and told about my first Christmas away from home as a young missionary in Germany. I believe, however, that Rachel was the star of the evening.

The children listened with wide-eyed amazement to every word. Of course, Rachel has always been a "star" in my life in everything she does.

Thus began my journal entry that very special Christmas. In view of the lush green trees and shrubbery, the heat and constant steam-bath humidity, we had difficulty realizing that it was the Yule season, but it was a time of blessings in super-abundance. Only by reviewing the events recorded late each night in my journal could I believe all that had transpired, even within the preceding two weeks.

Ghana! Absolutely incredible! Back now at our home in Enugu, Nigeria, I recalled that first remarkable baptism in Ghana over and over. I could scarcely close my eyes without seeing the dazzling ocean, the sun, and all those people arrayed in white upon the shore. I saw dark faces filled with light, eyes rich and lustrous, smiles gleaming and white, full of jubilation.

Afterward we had ordained a number of brethren to the Aaronic Priesthood, organized the Cape Coast Branch, and set apart its leaders—J.W.B. Johnson as president with James Ewudzie and Edward Ewusie as counselors and John Cobbinah as clerk. Sister Naomi Ogoe had become Relief Society president, and Lowell Diamond was called as district president with John Waby as his first counselor.

It had not ended there, however. The previous night ten additional prospective members had called at Brother Johnson's home in tears, having arrived late from a distant village on foot. I assured him that another baptism would be held the next day, little realizing that a total of thirty-six more would enter the waters, all having been interviewed and found worthy.

That same day we headed west by taxi only to have it break down, and had to finish our fifty-mile trip along the coast to Takoradi by bus. There we met a large and handsome woman named Rebecca Mould, known throughout that area as the "Mormon Prophetess." After a lengthy discussion regarding the true Church and the role of the priesthood, Rebecca had consented to relinquish the leadership of her congregation, and the next morning 124 people were baptized at beau-

With the Cape Coast Branch presidency (l. to r.): James Ewudzie, first counselor; Joseph William Johnson, president; Edward Evans Ewusie, second counselor; John Hill Cobbinah, clerk.

tiful Sekondi Beach nearby. We then organized the Sekondi Branch, Western Region, Ghana, with Sister Mould as president of the Relief Society.

The Sekondi church building was owned by Sister Mould, and that night before our return to Cape Coast I noticed a weathered sign outside at one end of the building, illuminated by a small overhead light. "The Church of Jesus Christ of Latter-day Saints—Founded in 1830," it read, and again my heart was filled to overflowing. Now the words of that sign had become authentic; the true and living Church had been established. During the past four days we had literally been blessed beyond compare, having organized two branches and baptized 249 people.

It was a demanding existence—difficult travel conditions, stifling heat, late nights, high expenses, scarcity of drinking water, and often we had to go all day long without a decent meal. At times we all were beset with stomach trouble, and within a space of several weeks I had lost twenty-five pounds.

Sign encourages Sisters Mabey (left) and Cannon as they and husbands at Cape Coast stop wait for bus that may or may not arrive. (This time it was a several-hour wait.)

The pace was taking its toll, yet all these things were insignificant compared to the spiritual harvest. Almost everything in terms of human resources seemed designed to advance the work. The people were invariably polite and helpful. During our weeks in Africa, in fact, I had not encountered a single case of prejudice or antagonism toward white people. More and more we had begun to feel that almost everyone we met was "golden," a promising prospect for baptism.

Back again in Accra, we had met on December 17 with President Johnson at the Waby residence. It was a Sunday afternoon, and President Johnson had brought eight new members, along with two investigators who desired baptism. He had come from Cape Coast that morning to teach a congregation there in Accra about the restored gospel, and had experienced much success. Despite the heat, President Johnson was wearing a suit and tie, perspiring, but full of enthusiasm. "You'll be interested to know," he said happily, "that about four hundred more people will soon be ready for baptism."

Exciting news, indeed, and it was a temptation in some ways to go forth and begin baptizing without restraint. Simul-

Aboh Branch sacrament meeting a few weeks after branch was organized.

taneously, it was more clear than ever that we should not proceed too fast and must now concentrate strongly on fellowshipping. "That's wonderful news," I said, "but tomorrow we must return to Nigeria for appointments there, and it is vital that we avoid moving ahead until our leaders gain the needed experience. In five or six weeks, though, we plan to return and continue our teaching. Afterward, we hope, we can conduct more interviews and hold a baptism."

All those present, including the two investigators, seemed pleased with the idea. Only one other matter seemed to concern them at the moment. "Now that we have been baptized," a young man asked, "is it necessary to wear white all the time?" Our reply relieved them considerably.

After that we had returned to Nigeria, and the following Sunday, December 24, had driven a hundred miles from our residence in Enugu to Aboh for sacrament meeting. It was a happy and special reunion, for President Anthony Obinna and the members there had been the first of God's children to enter the Church and become an organized branch in Black Africa. That day Rachel and I also commemorated our forty-fifth

Family of Francis and Rita Obinna typify the reverent Sunday-best approach to the Lord's day as they pose before moving off to church.

wedding anniversary. We had come a long way in space and time since joining hands across that altar in the Salt Lake Temple, but life had never been richer.

Eighty-one people, including the nineteen we had baptized on November 21, were present, more than the tiny chapel could contain. In consequence, our meeting was held outside under the shade of the palms and mango trees. It was well planned and presented, but there were, I must confess, occasional distractions. While the sacrament was being passed, a small boy hitched up his leg and extracted a thorn from one bare toe with his teeth. Minutes later, two people on motorcycles and one on a bicycle passed by directly between the sacrament table and congregation. I exchanged glances with my companions, joining in the struggle to contain our surprise and amusement. Hazards of an open-air meeting, I supposed.

Afterward, the entire congregation broke into song quite spontaneously, it seemed—a lively gospel hymn to the accompaniment of much hand clapping and loud, rhythmic drumbeats. "I have Jesus, the Son of God—why should I fear— why should I worry?" The words were repeated over and over in a primitive, throbbing chant, and soon the singers had risen to their feet, singing, shuffling, and swaying in a large circle— much like what we called a conga line back home.

Certainly the meeting deserved high marks for enthusiasm, and we had no desire to ridicule. While discussing the matter with President Obinna afterward, we stressed our appreciation for the culture and traditions of his people and the fact that they were part of a meaningful heritage. It was also essential, however, to explain what kinds of activities were appropriate for a sacrament meeting. These suggestions he and his counselors accepted with humility. "After all," he reminded us, "this is what we have been waiting for all these years—continued guidance and instruction."

CHAPTER TWELVE

Praising God

I t was a remarkable prayer, unlike any I had ever heard. The man offering it paused every few lines, deferring to the congregation of some two hundred members, many of whom would then stand and pray aloud simultaneously as moved upon. In consequence, dozens of these petitions were constantly rising in an atmosphere of great confusion. So, at least, it seemed for those of us who did not speak Efik, the language of that area, and so it must have seemed in some ways to everyone, with that many voices coming all at once. Only the Creator himself could have sorted it all out.

The date was December 30 and, as we had promised B. J. Ekong and his people, we were attending their two-day religious conference in the town of Eket (some six hours by car south of Enugu near the Bight [Bay] of Bonny). The gathering was impressively scheduled as "The Annual Convention of the Church of Jesus Christ of Latter-day Saints Mission, Ikot Ekong District," and the program, involving four lengthy sessions during a space of three days, was presided over by District Leader M. Daniel Essien. We were now in the beginning phase of a program that had started rather conventionally, by our own standards, with an opening prayer and hymn.

From then on, however, it acquired a kind of color and enthusiasm that we had never before witnessed.

Following the group prayer, a choir of nineteen young men and women sang in English a hymn titled "We Welcome You." This beautiful and harmonious selection was followed by an interlude simply titled "Choruses," which involved a lot of loud chanting, hand clapping, and drumbeats. Meanwhile, almost everyone in the congregation arose and began a swaying, shuffling dance much like the one we had witnessed earlier in the Aboh Branch sacrament meeting. In this case, however, they all sashayed up the aisles, depositing coins in a large collection platter.

The entire undertaking lasted for six or seven minutes and had barely finished when it began again in a kind of instant replay . . . then a third time, but now the man in charge of collections began to accept larger denominations and issue change. At that point I turned to Ted and whispered, "Very interesting, but it looks as if we have a lot of undoing to do." The collection festivities ended a few minutes later in a crescendo of praise-the-Lords and hallelujahs.

Then came more drumbeats, and members of the congregation, now seated, chanted and clapped with unabating gusto. During this part of the program, "Blessing of the House," a woman arose, dipped a large palm frond in a basin of water, and began swishing the saturated leaves about in a slow, measured rhythm, flinging water droplets upon the congregation. Those of us in front were also sprinkled, and one of her swishes caught me like a flurry of rain, saturating my open Bible enough that I had to wipe it dry with my handkerchief. Mr. Essien was seated beside me and explained that this procedure was designed to cleanse the recipients of their sins. In light of what had just happened, the need for cleansing in my own case must have seemed rather urgent.

Shortly thereafter, to our great amazement, the chanting, clapping, swaying, and drumbeats recommenced with additional trips to the collection platter—nine more, all told, including one for the children, in an undertaking that lasted nearly forty minutes! By now the four of us were exhausted merely from watching and almost deaf from the din. Sweat beaded our brows and upper lips and saturated our clothing, but the program was far from over. Next on the agenda was an enthusiastic sermon by the Evangelist B. J. Ekong, who focused his remarks upon the hanging of Haman and what he termed "the law of retribution."

The drummer had been hard at work throughout much of the session, and at last—two hours and twenty minutes after the opening prayer—he received a replacement and settled back to a well-deserved rest. Later still, the convention leader, the Reverend Essien, anointed 165 children and teenagers with oil, using a single drop in each case to form a small cross in their foreheads with his thumb.

Then eight expectant mothers, all apparently close to their delivery dates, came forward to kneel before the speaker's table and uncovered their midsections. The bare abdomens were sprinkled with "holy water" by two women who then probed about attempting to outline each unborn child with their hands and perhaps determine the presence of a heart-beat. A small cross was also formed over each navel with oil afterward, an act probably designed to bless the infant within.

The entire undertaking was unlike anything I had ever en-countered, a bit disconcerting at first, but by no means repug-nant. From my own point of view, in fact, it was rather moving and heartwarming—especially in a day and age when in many countries the lives of unborn children are frequently con-sidered of little value.

The meeting lasted some four hours, with three more that length to follow over the next two days—a hot and exhausting regimen. Even so, we all considered the experience very bene-ficial, affording valuable insight into the customs and religious traditions of these remarkable people. Never had we observed greater commitment or more undivided attention.

At the end of that session we learned from some of the con-vention directors that a number of their followers desired baptism and that a service had been planned for five o'clock the following morning. In response, however, Elder Cannon and I explained that the baptism would have to be postponed. Each prospective member would need further instruction in the gospel and a thorough interview, we told them. In con-clusion we also stressed that leaders in the Church do not receive salaries, to make certain that no one would seek membership for monetary reasons.

That evening we were introduced by our friend Daniel Ukwat to two young ministers who informed us that a total of ninety people from their two congregations were hoping to be baptized, a matter we promised to discuss with them following the next conference session on the morrow. "You know," Daniel confided afterward, "the first time you came here many of these people didn't believe you would ever return. After waiting so long . . ." He smiled and shrugged. "I guess it seemed unreal—as if they would wake up and find they had been dreaming. Now they know the truth."

Subsequent sessions of the present convention were similar in many ways to the first, but the second began with an official letter of welcome. Written and read by B. J. Ekong, it began as follows:

Dear Missionaries:

We the entire members of the Church mentioned above accord you a warm and hearty welcome on your maiden visit to us. Glory be to God for answering our fervent prayer.

We were like a son without a father and continued to live in misery and formidable suffering. However, we remained patiently with deep confidence that our sorrow would be over.

Your coming is significant and symbolic because it will mark the turning point and a great revival in this mission.

The letter went on to request that we make the Cross River State area a permanent missionary center in Nigeria, award scholarships to encourage the pursuit of higher education, and render financial aid for the building of churches and improving of economic conditions in general.

Such requests, I must admit, gave us certain misgivings, and yet it would have been unfair to assume that those involved were basically motivated by desires for financial gain. Their attitude was understandable in light of the fact that for many years missionaries of other churches in Nigeria had provided their followers material assistance, even building

Bassey J. Ekong.

schools and hospitals in some cases. In arising to respond, therefore, I did my best to explain our position as kindly but clearly as possible.

I concluded by bearing my testimony and was followed by Elder Cannon, who gave a powerful and convincing account of the Joseph Smith story. Fervent testimony was also borne by Brother Ime Eduok, the previously mentioned convert to the Church who had been baptized in Los Angeles. Subsequent testimonies from the congregation were uplifting, even through the mouth of an interpreter, and I was happy to note that those involved had not become disenchanted as a result of our refusal to promise direct material benefits. "I praise God continually," one man said tearfully, "that he has preserved me and my family for the coming of this great day." Another stated that some people had abandoned hope during their years of waiting and succumbed to the ways of the world, but he promised salvation to those who remained faithful. "Even though you can offer no economic assistance," he told us, "you come from God with the truth and are welcomed with joy. Great blessings lie ahead."

The convention ended on December 31, and we left promising to return soon to visit a number of villages in the area for teaching and baptismal interviews. Our friends, in turn, presented us with gifts—pineapples and entire stalks of bananas. A memorable conclusion, all of it, to the year 1978—a prelude to the great events ahead.

CHAPTER THIRTEEN

The Right People
in the Right Place

The night that followed, ironically, was rather miserable. The power went off as usual in our rooms at the government rest house at 11:00 P.M., and with it the badly needed fans and air conditioning. As a result, it was too hot and sticky to keep the windows closed, even to cover ourselves with a sheet. The mosquitoes buzzed and whined maliciously, feeding until satiated.

Once Rachel slapped her arm sharply and sighed. "Maybe we should have a blood transfusion every morning just to make up for what they steal during the night."

I laughed weakly and slapped my cheek, killing two enemies at once—great sport. "Well, at least we're taking our malaria pills." I yawned and thought of all the stress our wives were undergoing. As bearers of the priesthood, Ted and I were usually center stage, but our wives were a constant support, teaching and bearing testimony along with us in a spirit that was always moving, enduring hardship in the process without complaint.

We had brought cheese and bread with us from Enugu only to have it turn moldy, but thanks to our friends there was plenty of fruit. By now, in fact, I had eaten so many bananas I was beginning to feel like a monkey. Luckily, we had obtained meals of chicken and rice two different times during the past few days. Extremely hot meals, true, as a result of all the seasoning—but then, as I wrote in my journal, "What isn't hot around here?"

Happily, the tap water had been fairly dependable. With no means of boiling it, however, we were compelled to use disinfectant pills, a procedure that did little for the taste.

Even at that, we were gradually adjusting, a bit less staggered by the dramatic contrast in living conditions. If nothing else, it would make us appreciate the endless comforts and conveniences of home which we so easily took for granted. It would keep us humble.

Before returning to Enugu the next day we visited the village of Daniel Ukwat and attended part of a religious convention much like those in Eket. There we were treated to some magnificent singing and came away convinced that in time some of the great choirs of the Church would come from West Africa.

Awaiting us back in Enugu was a letter from President Faust, stressing the importance of providing adequate physical facilities for vast numbers of converts in places like South America and Africa, of developing the needed leadership, and insuring dedicated fellowshipping. He also asked for our recommendations in maintaining sound records and setting up tithing accounts.

"We are happy that you are well and busy," he wrote. "You are pioneers, and are the right people at the right place at the right time. It is historic."

A fine, encouraging letter, and we could certainly empathize with the concerns expressed. They had been matters of constant reflection and prayer on our part from the onset. Simultaneously, we continually had to reckon with the one other great and undeniable truth: The genie was now out of the bottle—there was no way of putting it back. The gospel had come to Black Africa, and it was extremely difficult asking those with honest testimonies, whose faith had been stretched for so many years, to wait longer now that we were actually in their midst. Above all, it was fast becoming clear that we needed more missionaries, dedicated couples well seasoned in the gospel, capable of organizing, instructing, and providing sound leadership training. Although Sister Janath Cannon was doing an excellent job as clerk, the task of record keeping itself would soon become overwhelming, even if we were to proceed with the baptisms far more slowly. Meanwhile, we would surely hearken to the counsel of our leaders in Salt Lake City and seek constant direction from the Spirit in building a firm and lasting foundation.

January 11, 1979, we set out for Calabar on a mission of great historical significance, convinced after much planning and prayer that the entire future of the Church in the Cross River area would rest upon our actions in the immediate future. We spent much of our time the next two days visiting villages and investigators in the area, and on the following evening we met with Ime Eduok and Daniel Ukwat back in Eket. Even though we had worked periodically with each of these men over the past two months, Elder Cannon and I felt that the time was now at hand for further, highly searching interviews. The results were most gratifying. Both men were thirty-six years old, devoted to their families, esteemed leaders among their people, and filled with strong testimonies of the true gospel. Both were also successful and respected in their vocations—Brother Eduok as a business executive, Daniel Ukwat as a schoolteacher. Although he had yet to be baptized, Daniel had studied the Church at length and was prepared for membership.

"We have met with you brethren this evening for some very important planning," I told them, "planning with regard to baptisms in this area over the next few days, but also re-garding the organization of what is known in the mission field as a district." Elder Cannon and I then outlined at length the overall organization of the Church and explained that branches in outlying areas are similar to wards in those places where the Church is more firmly established. Districts, we explained, are much like stakes.

"Our plan, brethren," I continued, "is to organize the Cross River State District—an arm of the Church which will embrace all of the branches we hope to establish within the entire Cross River State."

Both men watched us intently, nodding from time to time, their countenances full of understanding and inquiry. "But, of course," Elder Cannon added, "we won't be able to organize this district fully until we have several branches and until we have established strong leadership at those levels."

"That's correct," I agreed, "but we feel that it is time to begin—that the Lord has called you, Brother Eduok, as his district president, and you, Brother Ukwat, to be his first counselor. A second counselor will be chosen as soon as the right person is baptized and available." Both men nodded gravely, saying little at first, but their humility and willingness to accept came through strongly. "We are sure you understand the tremendous responsibility coming with these positions," I said. "In the very near future many members of God's true church will be looking to you for guidance, and we know that you will set examples that are always above reproach."

"We understand," Brother Eduok replied quietly. His eyes glistened. "I will gladly devote my life to the Church and even die for it, if necessary." Daniel Ukwat nodded emphatically, stating that he too was willing to make any sacrifices required, then smiled. "There is one small matter that we should attend to first, though, if I am not mistaken."

We all laughed. "Yes," Ted said, "something called baptism. That's another reason for the present meeting." In the discussion that followed, plans were laid to hold baptisms over the next two days in several of the surrounding villages, bringing in as always only those who had been interviewed and had proven themselves worthy and strong in the faith. We had worked with these people and taught them from time to time earlier, and felt certain that it was time for action.

The next morning, anticipating a long day ahead, we indulged ourselves in a rare breakfast of ham, eggs, and toast at the government rest house. It was a great treat, for everyone but me. "What a delight," I remarked happily. "What a change from bananas and cheese!" Hungrily I settled down to business, but in the process of carving my ham noticed that a large brown worm had arrived there ahead of me. Somehow it had survived the frying pan and was bent on making an escape. Luckily, the others failed to notice my little predicament, and I proceeded to eat around it. I made no mention of the incident until some time later, in fact, not wishing to destroy the appetites of my companions.

Otherwise, the day was magnificent. At the home village of Daniel Ukwat, a place called Idung Imoh, we found many people awaiting us. We interviewed fifty-one of them search-ingly, not only to insure that they were converted but also to identify potential leaders.

The baptism was held afterward in a small stream in the nearby jungle. Our prospective members had dug out a font deep enough to permit immersion, and the water sparkled constantly with brightly colored little fish. A short distance away separate houses had been constructed of green palm leaves so that the men and women could change their clothes in privacy.

That afternoon we baptized all those interviewed, beginning with Daniel Ukwat, and confirmed them later at their meetinghouse. It was a humble little structure, plastered with mud and painted yellow, but it served the purpose, and the Spirit was present. Later still, in that same meetinghouse, we organized the Cross River State District, setting apart Brothers Eduok and Ukwat as arranged in our previous night's meeting and ordaining Brother Ukwat a priest. Brother Eduok had expressed a desire to wait and receive the Melchizedek Priesthood a little later, in the midst of his own family and village. In our final undertaking of the day we organized the Idung Imoh Branch with Joseph David Eshiet, a newly or-dained priest, as president.

A day later, January 14, in the village of Ekong, I laid my hands upon the head of President Eduok and conferred on him the Melchizedek Priesthood, ordaining him an elder. And thus, history was again made: Ime Eduok had become the first of God's black children in all of Africa to receive the Melchizedek Priesthood. Daniel Ukwat became the second, ordained under the hands of Elder Cannon, and both brethren were immedi-ately pressed into service.

Other baptisms followed that day in villages close by, with more organization to follow. Before the day was over, in fact, there were four branches of the Church within the Cross River State District, at Okom, Ekong, Anang, and Isighe. Four solid cornerstones, and a total of 182 new members. In the process, The Church of Jesus Christ of Latter-day Saints had acquired the use of four meetinghouses along with a good supply of benches, tables, and other accoutrements.

Late that afternoon, convinced that our work was completed for the present, we received word that at least two hundred more people were awaiting us in Ikot Eyo. With darkness approaching, however, attending to such a group was impossible. Furthermore, our schedule demanded that we return home promptly to Enugu. As a result, Elders Cannon and Eduok paid them a brief visit, explaining the situation and promising that we would return for further teaching and interviews the following month. Many of the villagers were saddened at this news, some a bit angry, but their attitude soon changed. In appreciation of our efforts they heaped us with chickens, several dozen eggs, and plenty of fruit.

Upon checking out of the rest house that evening, we were compelled to empty our pockets—every bit of change down to the last naira—in order to pay our bill. It was an exhausting six-hour return to Enugu in our recently acquired V.W. The car was old with plenty of tough miles behind it, and our travel homeward took us on and on over treacherous roads in the dead of night, but the marvelous events just past continued to sustain us.

"I hope," Rachel said, and her voice was muffled with weariness, "that those people who are still waiting won't feel too unhappy."

"It's quite a thing," Janath replied. "Where else in the whole world will you find two hundred people waiting like that, practically *demanding* baptism!"

We stared ahead, following the path of our headlights, knowing that many others were waiting all around us, "here and there and everywhere"—thousands all told, probably. But to everything there was a season. For now, we could run no faster.

CHAPTER FOURTEEN

An Apostle Arrives

The jet materialized in the sky well ahead of its roaring. It was no larger at first than a gray locust—but in place of the locust's high-pitched electric hum, it trailed a long, undulating roar as though moving down some vast invisible corridor from the north. Gradually it enlarged, turning silver, and flashing sunlight in a sky of mingled green and blue.

We watched as the jet began to circle, the body becoming long and tubelike—too long, it seemed, for the stubby, swept-back wings. Many people were there at the Lagos Air Terminal, a number of them awaiting that particular plane. Elder Cannon and I and the two young black men with us, however, watched the landing with particular anticipation. Perhaps we even held our breaths a little at the moment of touchdown, for we knew something the others didn't. Aboard that jet was an Apostle of the Lord.

That Apostle was our old-time friend Elder James E. Faust, and minutes later we spotted him as he emerged amid a long line of people descending from the aircraft. Only four months had passed since we had parted in Salt Lake City, but so much had happened in the meantime that it seemed far longer. What a pleasure it was to see that handsome, rugged countenance once again and the broad smile! And to our joy his wife, Ruth,

Expectant crowd in Eket await arrival of missionaries who will baptize them.

had accompanied him, a lady of much charm, always pleasant and sociable.

Despite all their warmth and vitality, the Fausts were weary from their long trip. Fortunately, they were able to get through customs quickly, and the four of us boarded a plane soon afterward for the hour's journey to our home in Enugu. There we enjoyed a delicious meal prepared by Janath and Rachel, and later the Knudsen family came by to shake the hand of an Apostle.

Afterward Ted and I met with Elder Faust to discuss the challenges of Church organization and leadership in that land and the possibility of dividing Nigeria and Ghana into two separate missions. By 10:00 P.M. we had barely begun on the subjects that needed to be covered during Elder Faust's projected three-day visit. We were scheduled to leave rather early in the morning, however, for a trip to the Aboh Branch, and all of us needed sleep.

Elder Faust's letter advising us of their visit had arrived late, like nearly all mail in Nigeria—so late, in fact, that we had been compelled to reschedule our anticipated baptism of approximately two hundred people in the village of Eket. That important undertaking would be attended to soon, though, and meanwhile we planned to conduct a smaller baptism at Aboh, much nearer Enugu, so he could participate.

Shortly after our arrival there, Elder Faust was preaching to an excited and attentive gathering in the branch sacrament meeting, and those brethren whom we had recently ordained to the Aaronic Priesthood performed their assignments very effectively. Although a few discreet suggestions still needed to be offered afterward, the Saints at Aboh had made great progress in conducting sacrament meetings as prescribed by the Church.

The highlight of that special hour, of course, came with Elder Faust's address, and his words were full of encouragement and love—strong and direct yet unassuming. Despite his high calling, like all our General Authorities, he was one of us, full of humility and understanding. "When it will happen," he said, "I can't be certain; it will depend upon the faithfulness of people like yourselves, and it will require a Church membership of about one hundred thousand people. But one day," he paused, then continued, "there will be a temple in Africa."

Elder Faust went on to explain the vital role of temples in our lives and stressed the need of building a solid foundation for the Church in that land. Divine authority and the keys of the priesthood, he added, resided within the restored gospel alone. Then he concluded with his blessing and special testimony as a witness of Jesus Christ.

Five more people were interviewed for baptism that day, and during the interim several of us accompanied Elder Faust on an inspection of the building site donated by the Obinna family to the Church. "This truly is beautiful," he remarked, "a wonderful spot to build a chapel." And indeed it was—a level tract of farmland and forest interspersed with graceful palms that seemed to have already been ordained for that very purpose. "It may well be," Elder Faust said, "that we will construct meetinghouses here in Africa much like those in South America. Such buildings can be built in stages on a module basis with an initial expenditure of only ten to fifteen thousand dollars."

Later that day he had the pleasure of baptizing his first members of the black race. Five young men were immersed in

At mission home in Enugu, Nigeria: Elder and Sister James Faust (center) with the missionary couples.

the river at that same historic spot where President Anthony Obinna and eighteen others had been baptized three months earlier.

"That was a wonderful experience," Elder Faust later told us. "No one has ever listened to me more intently than those young men did when I talked to them about the Church before their baptism. You have the beginnings of a very strong branch here in Aboh. Brother Obinna and the others who have been called are beautiful people with great commitment and leadership potential."

Back in Enugu late that night we discussed the future of the Church in Nigeria and Ghana, and I stressed the urgent need of calling more missionary couples to serve in those countries. A day later we bid Elder and Sister Faust farewell at the Lagos Air Terminal. It was a reluctant good-bye, one that left us feeling a bit empty, but the Lord's errand is an unending one for his Apostles, and people are waiting everywhere.

That night I recorded the events of our three days together, then leafed through my journal reviewing what had happened over the past few weeks. As usual, there was that sense of amazement—so much in so brief a time:

January 21—Parking beside the road on our way to Rivers State and praying with Elder Cannon in a grove of cashew trees for guidance . . . holding a baptism near Ogbogu Village two days later, the great river slumberous in the mist, spotted here and there with the dim outlines of tiny fishing boats. As our first candidate had entered the water, spectators along the shore had fallen silent. An ancient fisherman, paddling his frail dugout toward us, had stopped rowing, removed his broad-brimmed hat, and waited, head bowed.

January 24—An exciting letter from Brother J.W.B. Johnson, our branch president in Cape Coast, Ghana. It read in part as follows:

"Since you left us we have been very serious with the teaching of the doctrines of the Church. We have extended the teaching program to Fosu, Manso, Accra, Nkamfoa, Nchaban, etc. During my visit to these places, I realized that the people there have a growing interest in the doctrine of the Church and are also getting ready for baptism. Following are the number of people in various stations who are ready for baptism:

Fosu/Manso	180
Accra	150
Nchaban	80
Cape Coast	36
Nkamfoa	20
	466 Total"

We will certainly have to visit Ghana again soon. If only there were more of us!

January 26—A visit with President Johnson in the Cape Coast Branch, reviewing, among other things, the thorough and neatly kept minutes of their sacrament meetings recorded by his clerk, Brother John Hill Cobbinah. Curious amusement over a small notation regarding the Word of Wisdom:

"The President quoted a piece from the Doctrine and Covenants, section 89 to support this. He said, among other things, that we should not drink wine, coffee, and tea, or eat Quaker Oats; neither should we smoke tobacco."

Excellent program and minutes, we told President Johnson, but why the injunction against oats? In reply, we were referred to the section just cited, verse 17, which reads, "wheat for man, and corn for the ox, and oats for the horse." We rectified the problem by referring him to the preceding verse, which states that "all grain is good for the food of man." Oats, in short, are especially good for horses but by no means bad for human beings, we explained. "Fine, fine," came the reply. "We will inform the members in our next meeting that they can begin eating rolled oats again." Such was the spirit of those good people. Even though rolled oats had been a staple part of their diet, they were ready to make any sacrifice necessary without question. "We want to do what is right. Just let us know." That was it, in essence, and the attitude never ceased to inspire us.

January 27—Another baptism at a rocky cove near Cape Coast, Ghana—twenty-nine new members, bringing the total number of converts in that area to 152. Retiring to the seclusion of some nearby bushes following the service, I began changing my wet clothes only to discover that I had been followed by three young "men-in-waiting," who discreetly turned their backs but reached out at times to receive my sopping apparel. Afterward they actually insisted on cleaning the sand from between my bare toes, then put on my socks and shoes, tying the laces fastidiously in neat, careful bows. "Is that satisfactory?" one inquired earnestly. "Is there anything else we can do?" Very satisfactory indeed, I replied—a little embarrassed perhaps at being treated so royally, but touched and grateful.

Returning to our quarters at the University of Cape Coast, we passed a stand of immense palms along the seashore. Several boys with machetes were climbing them and picking the coconuts, which they dropped to the sand below. We stopped long enough to purchase a few and celebrated by quaffing the "milk" inside.

That same day we had visited Nkamfoa nearby. There we met with the village chief, a young man who truly seemed joyful over our arrival and bid us an enthusiastic welcome. At dusk we held a meeting in the village square. Nearly three hundred people were there, including our fifty-member Church choir and a number of other members from Cape Coast. Elder Cannon and I both spoke at length and bore testimony, along with our wives, and gradually our audience was enveloped in the moonless night, virtually absorbed in darkness. Our only light was shed by the stars and a few tiny lanterns here and there among the congregation. A strange and moving experience, a time of enchantment, and afterward fourteen people requested baptism. Many of those assembled had walked for three or four miles and now returned as they had come, making their way home in the velvet darkness without the slightest hesitation or complaint.

January 28—More baptisms at the beach cove. This time, however, Elder Cannon and I merely served as witnesses, having perched on a nearby rock to see and hear better. President Johnson and his two counselors, now priests in the Aaronic Priesthood, performed the immersions as instructed, and thus occurred another first: the first baptisms performed by our black brethren in the entirety of Africa. Six brethren also received the Melchizedek Priesthood that day, among them J.W.B. Johnson and James Ewudzie, who were then set apart as district president and branch president respectively.

January 29—Spent much of the morning outside Fosu searching for an appropriate baptismal site with the aid of President Johnson and our cab driver. The area was some distance from any large water sources, and it was also the dry season, a fact that complicated our problem. At one point we discovered a streambed with enough water, but the water was far too swampy. Later we were told of a small stream about a mile from town that would supposedly be adequate, but upon arriving there with our prospective members, we found it was too shallow. It was also lined with boulders, and a layer of rocks within the streambed appeared to make any digging impossible.

After a lot of fruitless discussion, Elder Cannon and I retired to a grove of rubber trees to pray for guidance. We were already dressed in our baptismal clothes, and Elder Cannon offered the prayer. Kneeling there beside him in the silent, sun-patched forest, I rested a hand on his shoulder, feeling strongly the bond of brotherhood between us, the presence of the Spirit. Arrayed in white, head bowed, my companion was indeed a man of God and certainly looked the part.

Guidance came promptly. Upon rejoining the others, we immediately discovered a place where a font could be excavated, and all of us went back to the village. Elder Cannon then returned to the baptismal site to perform the excavation with the aid of two men bearing a bucket and shovels, while I remained behind to complete our interviews.

Eventually, by dint of much effort, our diggers excavated a shallow trench about seven feet long and three feet wide, but the following baptisms were rather difficult. In order to be completely immersed, the candidate had to be in a sitting position with the person performing that ordinance kneeling beside him. The water was actually so

shallow that an assistant was also on hand to hold the
candidate's feet down and prevent his toes from surfacing.
Awkward, yes, and rather unorthodox, but the only possible procedure, and one way or another each new candidate was submerged as required.

Sixty-nine new members were added to the fold that
day, including the parents and brothers of Emmanuel Bondah. President Kimball had read excerpts from a letter
written by this young man at our Regional Representatives
meeting the preceding fall. Away at school during the time
his family was baptized, he received that ordinance the following day.

January 31—Rachel's birthday, and I had penned the
following in my journal:

"Rachel is a great missionary, an excellent companion,
easy to get along with and understanding. When the going
gets rough she is right there with her loving arms around
me, speaking words of encouragement and cheer. Despite
the physical discomforts she never complains, and her
morale is always high. The Lord has blessed me with the
best wife on earth, and I love her very much. I know of no
one I would rather be with throughout all eternity!"

That morning we awakened in our quarters at the University of Cape Coast to the singing of countless birds. In
the evening we journeyed to Sofokrom, where, in a humble
little meetinghouse with walls of bamboo and palm leaves
for a roof, we interviewed forty-six people for baptism. By
then night had fallen, but our work was not completed.
Elder Cannon, President Johnson, and I journeyed about
half a mile on foot in the darkness to visit the village chief.
A young man and schoolteacher, he was arrayed in the
heavy robes of his office and sweated profusely, constantly
wiping his brow. The perspiration, however, did not
dampen his enthusiasm. Upon hearing of our proposed
baptismal services for the coming day, he stated that
anyone preaching faith in Christ was most welcome in his
village. In addition, he actually promised to provide land
for a meetinghouse, building materials, and money if
necessary!

The following morning we journeyed single file through some hill country to the Anankwa River, and this time there was no problem with scarcity of water. It was, in fact, so deep only a short distance from shore that we inserted two long poles in the mud to help us maintain our balance and keep from plunging into the river over our heads. Three sisters were practically carried from the water in a state of emotional exhaustion following their baptisms, and we administered to one of them to calm her nerves.

Forty-nine members were baptized there, and a number of the local brethren who now held the priesthood assisted, performing the ordinance under our direction. One of them even baptized his own wife, a joyful event for all of us. That same day we organized the Sofokrom Branch.

Later we also received a visit from John Osei, our lawyer friend from Ghana. Brother Osei had recently been in Salt Lake City and returned bearing a very special letter of greeting to the Saints of West Africa.

"Jan. 24, 1979

"Beloved Members:

"We greet you with affection and best wishes. We promise you great joy and happiness as you mature in this cause. Millions of members of The Church of Jesus Christ of Latter-day Saints bid you welcome.

"We encourage you to work closely with the official representatives of the International Mission of the Church, Brothers Rendell N. Mabey and Edwin Q. Cannon, Jr., in building the Church in that great land. I extend my blessings and pray for your continued spiritual development. God bless you.

> "Faithfully Yours,
> Spencer W. Kimball
> President"

The letter had been given to Brother Osei for hand delivery to us as the most expeditious means of broadcasting President Kimball's message to members throughout Ghana. Certainly it was heaven sent, arriving at a time when we were being pressed with many questions by our new members as to priesthood authority.

Members at Sekondi, for example, were concerned over the fact that Sister Rebecca Mould could not sit on the stand with the branch presidency during Church meetings. Sister Mould was not only Relief Society president, but had founded the group that called themselves Latter-day Saints long before our arrival. Her supporters reasoned—understandably, considering their limited knowledge of Church organization and priesthood authority—that an exception should be made in her case. She also owned the church building and grounds, and members had begun holding meetings on Wednesdays and Fridays to collect funds "for her maintenance and well-being." During those meetings drums were frequently played as well because our new converts did not want to abandon their traditions.

In response, we informed those involved that we, too, would hate to see their traditions lost and that drums were appropriate for some kinds of meetings but not for those held on the Sabbath. As for collections, members there were enjoined to abandon the procedure they had been following, to observe faithfully the law of tithing and pay fast offerings and a budget. Sister Mould could then receive a fixed rental from the latter source for the use of her building.

Members of the branch presidency and others present during the meeting in this connection were pleased with our explanations and delighted over President Kimball's message, agreeing to make extra copies for distribution to the surrounding branches.

February 4—We attended services at the Sekondi Branch, and during the fast and testimony meeting I arose, taking Sister Mould by the hand and asking her to stand beside me at the pulpit. I began by bearing my testimony and afterward explained that Sister Mould possessed a powerful testimony of her own. "She has done much for the people of this area," I told them. "We love her, and she is one of God's choice daughters. When I interviewed her for baptism in December, she was told that in becoming a member of the true Church she could not hold the priesthood and that she would lose her job as a prophetess. Despite these things, however, she was true to her convictions

On a Ghana beach: Ready for baptism.

On the beach at Sekondi, Ghana, with new members.

and was baptized. We admire her faith and courage, as we admire your own. We promise you that endless blessings will come to all who follow God's words as revealed through his prophets."

We left the meeting with a positive spirit, feeling that all dissension had been dispelled. We would return shortly thereafter to Nigeria; our work in Ghana had been completed for the moment.

CHAPTER FIFTEEN

Where Miracles Never Cease

A large truck was parked near the roadside as I walked by. A man was at work beneath it, flat on his back, another one standing by to hand him tools. On a sudden impulse I squatted down, craning my neck for a better view, and called out, "Hey, is it cool under there? I hope so, because it's pretty hot out here." The man paused in his tinkering, and I pressed my advantage. "I'm a missionary, and if you're interested in religion—if you believe in Jesus Christ—I'd like to talk with you."

The man responded by crawling out from under his vehicle and struggling to his feet. He was big and muscular, covered with grime and grease, and held a hammer in one hand. Rather a forbidding spectacle, but both he and his helper listened with apparent interest while I explained my mission, leaving them a copy of "Joseph Smith's Testimony" with my name and post office address.

We had not as yet encountered large groups of investigators in Enugu, our home base, but I wanted greatly to establish a branch there soon and had, therefore, launched some experimental tracting. Thus far the effort had proven highly encouraging, and it seemed as if there was no limit to the interest in our message. In passing out tracts on the street corners we were rarely rejected; not one person in twenty ever turned us down. Waiting to cash a check in the bank, visiting the offices of business or government, we invariably found someone happy to listen.

On one occasion in the city of Umuahi, a considerable distance southeast of Enugu, we even managed some proselyting while changing a flat tire. We were in the midst of heavy traffic, and several people had stopped to offer assistance. As more help had assembled than we actually needed, I began passing out Church literature to our new friends. One of them, a man in a black uniform, told me that he was a fireman, and just before we left he drew me aside rather confidentially. "I am very impressed with what I've just been reading," he said, "and feel that I would like to join your church."

Upon learning that we were headed for Eket, some miles to the southeast, he brightened even more. "In that case," he said, "after traveling about thirty miles you will come to my home village of Oloko. Please stop there and introduce the people to your religion. I feel certain that they will also want to join."

Truly, miracles never ceased there in West Africa. An hour later we stopped at Oloko for a meeting with the fireman's wife, six children, and other relatives. One of his uncles was the local schoolmaster, and I informed him that we had journeyed halfway around the world to bring the restored gospel. I then presented him with a copy of the Book of Mormon, exhorting him to read it prayerfully. This he agreed to do, promising that he would explain it to the others and write us in Enugu if they desired more information.

Everywhere . . . everywhere . . . everywhere! People fairly clamored for the gospel. After checking into the hotel at Eket that evening we were met by two men who had come by motorcycle to ask if we would visit their village. One of them, a minister, informed us that approximately sixty people in his congregation desired to see us. They had been writing letters to Salt Lake City for some time, had read "Joseph Smith's Testimony," and were eager to learn more. Reluctantly, we explained that our appointment book was brimming over for the next three months, but provided them an ample supply of literature that they could be studying in the meantime.

At nine the following morning we assembled in a small church in the nearby village of Eyo where a choir of young people sang us a song of welcome. We then preached the gospel with Brother Sunday D. Ukpong, former minister and recent convert, acting as interpreter. Brother Ukpong had just reported that two hundred people were awaiting baptism in his own village of Imoh.

Present also at that meeting were several of our new branch presidents and other leaders from a surrounding area of thirty or forty miles in radius. Included among them were Brothers Ime Eduok and Daniel Ukwat, who like the others had come by prior arrangement to assist us in the proposed baptism.

Later, as Elder Cannon supervised the interviewing, I met with certain leaders who urged us to spend far more time in the Cross River State. All told, they said, twelve different groups had been awaiting the missionaries for some time. "Frankly," Brother Eduok informed us, "many of these people are becoming very impatient. They want to be baptized now!"

In response, I explained that we shared their concern and believed that more missionaries would be sent out by the Church soon. "Meanwhile, we hope that you will please be patient with us and understand that we are working as diligently as possible," I said, praying that they would empathize.

At 1:00 P.M. we proceeded to a stream close by and presided over a beautiful pre-baptismal service conducted by our local brethren. Our prospective members were assembled in a long line that descended from a hillside into the water. I waited there for them, smiling, feeling a sense of joy and fulfillment that knows no comparison, then extended my hand to the first candidate and commenced the baptisms. Elder Cannon and District President Eduok confirmed each one as he or she emerged from the stream. Thus we proceeded for nearly two hours, and that day 117 members were added to the Church.

A marvelous experience, but the afternoon was brutally hot even though we had selected a shady area. Upon leaving the water, I could scarcely maintain my balance. The landscape seemed to be rotating slowly—trees, clouds, and blue sky—like part of a gigantic stage setting. I was told that Rachel had taken ill and fainted. "She was just sitting here beside us,"

Eager candidates line up for baptism.

Ted related, "and suddenly she passed out for a minute. I wanted to let you know, but Rachel refused to allow it."

"Absolutely not!" Rachel exclaimed. "I had Ted administer to me instead, and I've been feeling perfectly fine ever since."

We arrived at our quarters that night exhausted and nearly famished, having dined on nothing for lunch but a banana and half a bottle of soda pop each. As on the preceding night, there was not a drop of water in our rest house, and we were compelled to fetch a bucketful from the Qua River two hundred yards away, then purify it with tablets we carried for that purpose.

As if to compensate for the lack of water indoors, it rained hard during the night to the accompaniment of wild flashes of lightning and claps of thunder. At one point we were almost rocked from our beds by a mighty, booming concussion, as if a jet plane had broken the sound barrier directly overhead.

The following day was fast Sunday, and sixty-seven more people were baptized, bringing the total number of new members since that previous afternoon to 187. We then organized the Eyo Branch, Cross River State District, and late that afternoon President Ime Eduok asked me to draft a legal paper that his attorney could file in Lagos, the Nigerian capital, to help strengthen Church recognition throughout that country. This I was happy to do, penning the document in my own handwriting since no typewriter was available. Although our position legally was more secure now, I had remained uneasy over the matter, and thought it might well prove helpful to have a native Nigerian lawyer acting on our behalf.

On March 9, a few days after returning from the Cross River area, Rachel and I made one of our occasional visits to the native market to purchase some birthday presents. Such markets are remarkable places and function as the heart of a complex and dynamic system of international trade. Many of them sprawl on and on for blocks and contain almost everything imaginable: shoes, china, clothing, furniture, spices, perfume, medicines for virtually every malady, fruits and vegetables, live poultry . . . the list seems endless.

There in Enugu as many as ten thousand sellers might be assembled on a given day, but almost every large village boasted markets along similar lines, all having one selling stall after another with nothing but dirt floors—many of them mere lean-tos with palm-leaf roofs. Visiting or passing such places, we often saw women walking along with great piles of goods on their heads and, at times, a small stool inverted on top of everything—something to sit on while dealing with prospective buyers.

The demand for consumer goods in Nigeria is substantial. Even with an average income of only twenty dollars per month, a man can save enough on occasion to buy a tin roof for his home, a wristwatch, or a transistor radio. In addition, an expanding middle class, including the civil servants, teachers, and businessmen, adds greatly to the economy by purchasing such items as refrigerators, record players, and motorcycles. At the upper end of the economic spectrum are those who make enough to throw lavish parties and live in "real style."

Regardless of socio-economic level, however, most of these people, from the menial laborer to the high government official, were interested in our message. The field in this case was black, not white, but it was indeed "already to harvest."

CHAPTER SIXTEEN

Discovery in a Print Shop

G od Is Love," the sign on the print shop wall read. The carbon copy of my latest report to Salt Lake City had been so faint that I had gone there to the little shop in Enugu for a better duplicate.

Two men and a woman were seated on stools behind a makeshift counter, and one of them took my report into the back room to reproduce it. "That's an interesting sign," I observed. "Do you really believe what it says?"

The two remaining employees glanced at me with surprise. "Yes, certainly," the man replied.

"And you are interested in religion? You believe in the divinity of Jesus Christ?" Both of them nodded and replied at once, yes, indeed they did.

"Well," I smiled, "I'm glad to know that. I happen to be a missionary from America and have something you might like to read." Extracting a copy of "Joseph Smith's Testimony" from my leather carrying case, I handed it to the man, who was seated closest.

The woman, however, looked disappointed. "Don't I get one too?" she asked, deftly snatching the tract from her companion's hand.

"Why, surely," I chuckled, "you already have one," then handed the man a copy of "Which Church Is Right?" It was time now for an explanation. "I'm a representative of The Church of Jesus Christ of Latter-day Saints," I told them, "and I have come all the way from Salt Lake City, Utah, halfway around the world—"

Just then the first man returned abruptly from the back room. "Did you say, 'The Church of Jesus Christ of Latter-day Saints'?" he inquired, and stared at me in fascination.

"Yes, I did," I replied.

"Do you happen to have a copy of the Book of Mormon?"

I nodded, watching him intently. "Yes, I have one with me. Why do you ask?"

"I've wanted to read that book for a long time," he said, explaining that he had heard about the Church six or seven years earlier and had written to Salt Lake City for information. "I received some of the literature," he continued, "but was disappointed to learn that there was no one in Nigeria who could actually teach me more about the subject."

"Well," I smiled, "there is now." Reaching into my case again, I produced the book he desired, suggesting that he read Moroni's special promise in the last chapter. "After that read the first part of 3 Nephi 11, as well," I advised, "then start at the beginning and go all the way through." I also requested his name and address, stating that the book was merely on loan, that I would like to discuss it with him in the near future.

The man promptly complied with my request and astonished me by jotting down the following name: "Apostle Dr. Paul O. A. Ihuoma."

"Oh, you're an apostle, are you?" I said.

"Yes," he nodded, "I am."

"Well, now, that's very interesting," I mused. "I happen to know a few Apostles myself—it's nice to meet another one." Moments later I left, promising to return in a few days.

That night for a little diversion the Cannons and the Mabeys attended a movie, our first since entering Nigeria. The movie was an old-timer starring William Holden, and part of it had actually been filmed in Utah with a view of Mount Timpanogos in the background. The scene made us all a bit happy and homesick simultaneously, but throughout it all, I kept thinking of the "Apostle Paul," sensing that something very important lay ahead.

Our entertainment a day or two later was more traumatic. Ted was on the roof of our garage, having volunteered to repair a large hole with roofing material and tar. Inadvertently he stepped on a weak spot and went crashing through to land with a bang inside. Having observed his disappearing act from below, I rushed into the garage expecting to see my good companion sprawled on the floor and perhaps badly injured. He was standing there when I arrived, however, rubbing one elbow, scraped and bruised, decorated with tar and somewhat shaken, but otherwise all right. Fortunately, he had landed on the roof of our car, bounced to the hood, then slipped to the floor, taking his "downfall" in stages.

"Are you okay?" I asked.

Ted grinned uncomfortably. "I think so," he winced and inspected the smears of sticky blackness on his arms and shirt. "Tarred a little . . . but not feathered."

Two days later, March 11, 1979, we learned via short-wave radio that Ghana's Accra Airport had been closed, her borders to be sealed for the next two weeks or so. This action had been taken because that country was devaluating the cedi. In consequence, we were compelled to postpone our trip there for the time being. Unfortunate, yes, but there was plenty to keep us busy in Nigeria for the next ten years. I'm sure we all felt that by now. As I had advised the Brethren in Salt Lake City earlier, it would be easy to keep many more missionaries well occupied in that land indefinitely.

Meanwhile, I visited Paul Ihuoma at the print shop again and arranged with him to attend our newly organized investigator classes.

March 15 found us hard at work once more in Cross River State, journeying from Calabar toward Eket. Reviewing our investigator file along the way, we noted the name of a Pastor Lawson Udonsah who apparently resided only a short distance off the main road in the village of Ikot Eba. Later that day we visited his home, and despite the fact that it was now four-thirty in the afternoon, he insisted upon summoning his congregation by ringing the meetinghouse bell nearby. By five o'clock about one hundred people had assembled. Among them was the village chief, brightly arrayed in his official robes and carrying a beautiful, intricately carved staff denoting his office of authority.

We spent forty-five minutes there preaching the gospel to a most attentive audience, knowing all the while that we would have to cut our visit short for an appointment in Edebuk a few miles away. Before leaving, however, we presented the chief with a copy of the Book of Mormon and distributed other copies and tracts to a number of others present.

The response was almost overwhelming, and upon being asked to return the following day, we reluctantly explained that it would not be possible for us to meet with them again until late May or early June. In the meantime, they were advised to study the literature we had left, those who understood English having been urged to read and explain it to the others. At that point we were surrounded and fairly inundated with requests for more reading material. "How do you turn down a pleading person with tears in his eyes," I later wrote in my journal, "begging for a copy of the Book of Mormon?" The fact was, however, we simply did not have enough for everyone and had to be selective. "Please share with each other," we exhorted, "please share. We promise to bring more with us next time."

We arrived in Edebuk for our seven o'clock appointment with moments to spare, but no one was at the meetinghouse. The only sign of life, in fact, was a lone figure approaching on foot along the darkening road. As he drew near we called to each other in greeting. It was the Reverend Geoffrey Samuel Assam, a schoolteacher whom we had met previously, and he looked tired. His bicycle had broken down, and he had been walking for nearly four hours—fifteen long miles from the school where he was employed to the little church where we had agreed to meet.

Gradually others emerged from the darkness, some of them carrying lanterns, and we could scarcely avoid wondering a little about their tardiness. Quite a contrast to our earlier meeting, but the Reverend Assam clarified the situation for us. "I hope you will be patient with these people," he said quietly. "Nearly all of them are farmers who must work until dark, then walk a long way home and change their clothes before coming to church." Such dedication was surely impressive, and I recalled at the time another branch where members met in their chapel each morning at five o'clock for group prayer. Some of them had to travel quite a distance on foot, but they were convinced that the effort was worth it, the best way possible to begin their day.

Once again Elder Cannon and I spoke, along with our wives, extending greetings from our prophet, explaining the Apostasy, the Restoration, and other fundamentals. The Reverend Assam interpreted for the entire time since very few of those present spoke English, and we all concluded with fervent testimonies. "I have been a member of this Church for sixty-two years," I said, "and we all know it is true. If that were not so, why would we travel twelve thousand miles and labor from early morning until late each night to bring the people of Nigeria this joyful news?"

When I had finished, the Reverend Assam said that one of his assistants wished to address us. Arising slowly, the man bowed and expressed his appreciation. "Our people are greatly moved by your words," he said. "We are touched in our hearts by the Spirit and know for a certainty that you have been sent by our Father in Heaven." Pausing for a moment, he glanced at the congregation. All of them—men, women, and children —were watching him expectantly, eyes glowing in the dim and flickering rays of the lanterns. "I am very confident that everyone present would like to be baptized as soon as possible."

As always, however, we were compelled to hold back the flood, stressing the importance of having those present read the literature and study the doctrine. Our present responsibilities would likely prevent us from establishing any more branches until additional missionaries were sent from Salt Lake City, we explained. In any event, I concluded, we would return in June to provide further instruction.

Back at the Qua River rest house that night, I penned the following in my journal, trying hard to articulate an ever-growing anxiety for all of us:

> I really am concerned that we are extending our work too thinly now and must rest for a season to regroup and perfect our records and organization. As yet, because of our

isolation, we have not received any membership record forms from Salt Lake City. Our records are just on paper lists—and membership in these two lands should exceed one thousand by day after tomorrow.

Physically, life was often miserable. I was rapidly losing weight as well as my appetite, and at times Ted, for all his vigor, looked as though he had been drained of blood. Rachel and Janath fared little better, if at all. We were all becoming debilitated from living on the run, and from the endless heat and humidity. We tried our best never to complain, however, to keep our spirits up in times of trial. "We know the Lord needs only those who have gone through the refiner's fire," I wrote, "but it sure gets hot!"

CHAPTER SEVENTEEN

The Conversion of Paul

March 20, 1979

Dear Clegg, Mike, Charles, Sarah, Rachel, Elizabeth, and Emily:

Recently I met a man by the name of Sunday Daniel Ukpong in the village of Ukobo. We have now baptized him and his people, and yesterday he became a branch president.

As Grandmother Mabey and I visit the Nigerian people in their little humble homes, we often ask ourselves—Why do we have so much and they so little? We are no better than they. How did we get to the head of the line when worldly goods were handed out and these people are still in line waiting and waiting?

Sunday Ukpong has a wife and ten children and says he could wish for no more. A number of years ago he organized a little church and has helped many people understand the ways of their Father in Heaven without ever receiving any pay as their pastor. He makes his living as a trader selling clothes, and there is a rather large public market about six miles from his home where he does business.

It costs him ten naira (about seventeen dollars) per month for a license to sell there, and nothing is furnished —just a bare spot on the ground. Four days ago he walked the six miles to market in order to be there at eight in the morning, carrying all his goods as usual on his back. That day he was unable to sell a single item and returned home that evening with the same load of clothing. Can you imagine what it would be like to walk a total of twelve miles with such a load to and from work every day and sometimes never make a cent? Often, in fact, he goes to another market and has to walk twenty miles!

I asked him if he had a bicycle, and he told me that he has a very old one that is broken down, in bad need of repair. That was when I thought of you, my grandchildren, all of whom I love very much. I thought of all your fun toys, tricycles, and bicycles. I know how unselfish each of you is, and that you would gladly give some of your own possessions to assist him if you could. But how, for example, could you get a bicycle all the way to Nigeria?

Well, your grandmother and I have talked this over to see what we could do for you all to help. We thought and thought, and we also prayed. This is the plan—one with which we hope you will all agree. Bicycles are very expensive in Sunday's village, and recently we gave a friend 150 naira (about 250 dollars) to go to a big city two hours away called Calabar and purchase a new one. Then he took it to the village where Sunday lives and hid it in someone's home until we could give it to him.

A short time later your grandmother and I visited the Ukpong family. Sunday was there with his wife, and all ten children were gathered around. Their baby girl is just learning to walk, and while we were visiting she toddled over and touched my face. I think she was surprised to discover that white skin felt the same as black skin. When the bicycle was wheeled from its hiding place and Sunday saw it, his eyes grew big and round. He seemed to be stunned with surprise and wonderment. "What a beautiful bicycle!" he exlaimed. "Why is it here in my house?"

In reply, we told him, "We have some wonderful grandchildren at home. They are very kind and considerate, and

Sunday Daniel Ukpong and wife with his bicycle gift.

they want to help you get to work without walking so far for so many hours every day. Yes, Sunday, the bicycle is all yours," we told him, "a gift from each of our grandchildren to you."

I wish you could have seen the Ukpong family at that moment. Sunday's face lit up like a Christmas tree (though I don't imagine he had ever seen one). His wife put her hand to her own face in disbelief, and the children actually jumped and clapped their hands with glee. It was a beautiful bicycle with a light in front and a bell on the handlebars, and we asked Sunday to come outside and pose with it for some pictures, which he gladly did. It was the Sabbath, so he was dressed in his best clothes, and he also put on a little bowler hat. It made quite a picture and we will send you a copy later.

Now, how can you actually participate in this undertaking? I would like to suggest that each of you (and your friends also, if you wish) share in this mission and gift by giving up some little thing that you do not need every day for the next month. Then take the money which you were able to save as a result and give it to your Uncle Tom. He will add up each donation, and if that is not enough he will add some of grandfather's and grandmother's money to equal $250. He will then make out a check to the Church Missionary Fund and donate it to the Church. That way we can replace the money we borrowed to purchase the bicycle.

I feel sure that you will like this idea and find it lots of fun. Please write and tell us of your feelings about this and what you would like to do. We are very proud of each one of you and love you more than you will ever know. God bless you all.

> With love,
> Grandfather Mabey

Although we missed our families greatly, most of our letters home were brief and rather general. Soon our year-long mission would be half over, and much of my own letter writing, of necessity, involved official correspondence. The preceding message to our grandchildren, on the other hand, seemed to be worth the effort. Their response in the days to come proved it.

Meanwhile the days hurtled by like gazelle fleeing the wrath of a brush fire.

On March 21, the first day of spring at home, we were still sweating it out, literally and otherwise, there in Africa. The borders of Ghana remained tightly sealed, and a number of people there had died of heat prostration while waiting in the long lines to exchange their money. Any old cedis that were not exchanged for new ones by March 27 would become worthless. Commerce there was virtually paralyzed, and a number of people, including several high bank officials, had been arrested on charges of black-market activities.

I spent the following morning preparing a report letter for Elder Carlos E. Asay, who had replaced Elder Faust some time earlier as president of the International Mission. By now we had organized two districts in Nigeria comprising nine branches and seven groups. In Ghana there were two districts, four branches, and one group. That evening we held an investigators' meeting, and among those attending was my friend from the print shop, "Apostle" Dr. Paul O. A. Ihuoma.

The morning afterward I visited Paul's place of employment with several letters I needed to have reproduced. He had requested that I visit him there to determine a time and place for our next discussion. His employer took my order, however, and I waited for some time without success. Once I caught a glimpse of Paul in the back room and saw him wave; that was all. Eventually, unable to remain longer, I was about to leave when he appeared. "Here is something that might interest you," I said and handed him a copy of *Gospel Principles* without further comment. Paul's employer was still on hand, and I sensed a spirit of restraint. "See what you think of it," I added, "then come and see me if you wish to."

"Thank you," came the reply. "I'll just walk outside with you to say good-bye."

Once we had left the shop, I turned to him expectantly. "Paul," I said, "apparently you didn't want to discuss religion in front of your employer, but I hope you'll read carefully the book I just gave you. It's a good one. I have been praying about the matter and have a strong feeling that the Lord has brought us together. I want to testify to you again that my message is true."

Paul nodded solemnly, but his round, pleasant face emanated warmth. "I have been praying also," he replied, "and am convinced that you are right. My wife has just given birth to a child, but I have told her about you, and she feels just as I do. We want very much to help establish your church in Nigeria."

The next Sunday Rachel and I enjoyed a special evening with Paul, his wife, and their four little girls. It was then that we learned something of his background. A few months before his birth, Paul informed us, his father had made a promise and uttered a prophecy. "If the child is born well," he said, laying a hand on his wife's bulging stomach, "and if he is a boy, he will spend his entire life serving the Lord." As he grew older, the young Paul Ihuoma was trained to become a priest in the Catholic Church and planned to be ordained in Rome. Unable to raise enough money for his final training and preparation, however, he was rejected.

Saddened and highly frustrated, he sought to commit suicide through starvation. For seven days he remained in solitude, refusing to eat or drink and praying for the Lord to take his life. Finally, concluding that the Lord would not cooperate, he returned home. There, at the urging of a friend, he reluctantly consented to study the King James Version of the Bible and began attending Protestant services. In time he became a leader and self-styled "Apostle" with a large following. The night of our meeting, in fact, he showed us an astonishing photograph—Paul himself, clad in his ministerial robes, preaching to a congregation that must have numbered several thousand. Beside him were three other men, translating the words he spoke in English to different native tongues.

In 1971, while walking on a dusty street of Enugu, he noticed a crumpled scrap of paper and picked it up. A mere fragment torn from something larger, it contained the name and address of the Church in Salt Lake City and aroused his curiosity. A short time later he wrote to the address indicated and received several tracts along with the Book of Mormon. The latter was accompanied by a message from Brother Lamar Williams of the Church Missionary Department, explaining that no missionary work was anticipated for Nigeria at the time. That was the last Paul ever heard of the Church until I entered the print shop eight years later.

It was a fascinating account, although the final part left me somewhat perplexed. "But I thought you didn't have a copy of the Book of Mormon," I said. "That was why I loaned you one when we first met."

Paul smiled a bit sheepishly. "I asked you to give me a copy," he replied, "because I wanted to make absolutely certain that you were a representative of the LDS Church. I had read the book cover to cover long before."

The following day Paul attended our priesthood services at the Knudsen residence. We met outside in the shade of a blossoming plumeria tree, and the ground around us was strewn with delicate red and pink flowers that exuded a wonderful fragrance. From time to time petals drifted down to land upon our opened scriptures—a perfect blend of the aesthetic and spiritual, and certainly one of the loveliest Church meetings I had ever attended.

Paul O. A. Ihuoma in traditional tribal garb.

Several days later Paul was baptized at Udi Springs, not far from town. Emerging from the water we embraced like long-lost brothers in one of the great highlights of my mission. Paul Ihuoma was the first of our converts from Enugu itself, the firstfruits of direct tracting. He was truly the promise of things to come.

CHAPTER EIGHTEEN

Searching the Heart

The doctor sat there, head bowed, a look of attentive concentration on his face. He was in another world for a moment, the world of my heart, entered by means of a stethescope—and he was frowning ever so slightly. Straightening up, he removed the stethescope from his ears and regarded me gravely. "My friend," he said, "you definitely have a heart murmur, along with low blood pressure. In the past half year, you have lost twenty-five pounds." He paused, then continued, "Nigeria is no place for a man of your age and condition. If you and your wife were my brother and sister I would advise you to return to the United States right away. Frankly, I think it would be stupid for you to take your lovely wife back to Africa, everything considered."

A likable old gentleman, the doctor, bluntly honest yet kindly and pleasant. Nevertheless, I was beginning to wish I had never come to England for two weeks of recuperation. I had a superstitious feeling that my visit to the doctor was a mistake, that somehow a malady doesn't really exist until it is actually identified and acknowledged, given a place at the table.

"You need the diagnosis of a specialist, though," he continued. "In fact . . ." He paused again and began scribbling referrals on a note pad. "I'm sending you to several different specialists."

I raised my eyebrows and tried to act nonchalant, but inside I felt pretty hollow.

He continued to scribble. "A dermatologist, for one thing. You've been getting too much sun and may have a case of incipient skin cancer. Most important of all, of course, we need a more detailed check on your heart. That's why I'm sending you to a first-rate cardiologist."

"Well," I laughed, "I guess that should do for openers."

The dermatologist later treated several facial lesions with liquid nitrogen and decided that I could withstand the African sun a few months longer. The cardiologist, after X-rays and extensive testing, informed me that one of my heart valves had only two openings instead of the normal three—that I had probably been born that way—and that one valve was filling with calcium. "I wouldn't recommend surgery at the moment," he said, "but the condition bears careful monitoring. You need to avoid too much stress and should have a thorough check-up every two or three months."

He was hardly enthusiastic over my explanation that we had six more months left on a mission to West Africa. In the end, however, my X-rays were sent by Elder Robert D. Hales, president of the England London Mission, to Dr. Russell Nelson in Salt Lake City. A highly prominent cardiovascular and thoracic surgeon, Dr. Nelson had performed a critical heart operation on President Kimball and was former president of the Sunday School. Like so many others, I had great confidence in his expertise and advice.

Meanwhile, we telephoned Ted and Janath, who were then in Athens en route to Israel, attended church at the Hyde Park Ward, and had an enjoyable family home evening with President Hales, his wife, Mary, and twenty-six missionaries at the London mission home. To my surprise, I was asked to be the guest speaker. The Hales family, in fact, had insisted that we reside with them during much of our stay in England, providing us with the best of care and plenty of Mary's delicious home cooking.

At President Hales's suggestion, we also journeyed ten hours by train to Inverness, Scotland. The landscape with its moors and lakes, its winding rivers and forested hills, was magnificent. I had never seen so much wild game from a train window in my life: ducks, pheasants, grouse, rabbits, at least two hundred elk-like stags, and, to my delight, what appeared to be a timber wolf. Our only disappointment—no sign of the legendary monster at Loch Ness.

Back in London five days later, we received a much-appreciated telephone call from Dr. Russell Nelson, who informed us that the London doctors had diagnosed my condition very accurately. "The calcium deposit in your heart valve has undoubtedly built up over a period of many years, and it will be some time before the valve must be replaced," he told me.

"Well, that's at least encouraging," I said. "I want greatly to complete my mission if it's at all possible." I paused, reflecting. "If I were home, I certainly wouldn't be sitting around in a rocking chair for the rest of my days. I'd be hunting and fishing, riding horses, snowmobiles, motorcycles —sometimes even a tractor." Another pause. "If I *were* home, how long before you'd need to see me?"

"Oh," came the reply, "probably about six months, provided your condition remained stable."

"Wonderful," I said. "In that case, I'll complete the remaining six months of my mission, then pay you a visit."

Dr. Nelson chuckled. He understood my desire in a way the London physicians, for all their competence, never could.

"All right, Brother Mabey," he told me. "Just be careful. Don't overtax yourself. If you begin noticing any real symptoms—chest pains, increased shortness of breath, or faintness, take it as easy as possible and get in touch with me immediately. We may need to bring you home in that event."

Dr. Nelson failed to realize that "immediately" might actually mean several weeks for a person living in Africa, but I saw no advantage in pursuing the matter at that point.

The next night I dreamed of my hunting days in Southwest Africa and awakened in the darkness to recall a safari in Bechuanaland like none I had ever experienced before or since. In search of a wounded lion, we had suddenly found ourselves in the midst of an entire pride—a dozen plus of his relatives, all unhappy over our presence, several bent on revenge. During the long afternoon of tracking, in fact, we were actually attacked four different times and in each case escaped death thanks to the power of our rifles. The destruction of those great cats, in short, was strictly a case of survival, not merely my own but also that of my son Ralph, then only eighteen years old, our white hunter Mitch Spencer, and a number of native guides and trackers.

Throughout it all we continued to track the wounded male, knowing that we had an obligation regardless of danger or difficulty, and the climax to our experience came about an hour before sunset when the lion charged from behind an enormous ant hill. Our two quick shots missed the mark but turned him away, and he retreated into the tall grass with Mitch and his fundi (gun bearer) in pursuit. Yelling at Ralph to stay behind, I began running along the perimeter of a burned area, hoping to circle the island of grass ahead and gain a clear line of fire.

Moments later I heard three rapid shots followed by a terrible scream from the fundi. No choice but to keep running, and within only a few seconds I encountered the most awful sight of my life—a human being in the jaws of a monster. The victim was Mitch himself, and despite the terrible mauling, he battled valiantly, actually twisting the lion's ear with one hand and kicking at his vitals. Unable to place a shot under the circumstances, I bellowed wildly, hoping to distract the animal, and distract him I did. Dropping his prey, the lion whirled and came at me with a roar. All my senses, the entire surroundings, everything was consumed in the awful reality of that charging lion. There was a catapulting effect of mane, fangs, and hate-filled yellow eyes . . . and somehow the thunder of my rifle coming, it seemed, of its own accord.

At the onset of a great bound, not thirty feet away, the lion took a bullet squarely in the chest, whipped sideways, and received my second blast through the neck. With that, he pitched forward onto his chin, rolled over, and lay very quietly.

I was panting, shaking a little, and for an instant merely stared at our fallen enemy. But there was no sound, no motion, except for the ruffling of his mane in the hot African wind.

The attack had occurred in more burned area beyond the span of grass, and Mitch was so black from the ashes it was hard to tell him from one of the natives. One arm was badly mutilated, and his shoulder looked like singed hamburger with a hole in it the size of a handball.

We had left our vehicle, a large Land Rover, some distance behind, and Ralph was now sent with our natives to retrieve it while I attended to Mitch's wounds. Tearing my shirt into strips, I bandaged him to the best of my ability, but his condition was very serious. "Mitch," I said, "I'm not much of a doctor. Guess I've done all I can along that line for now, but I have a power that can make you well if you and I have the faith."

My friend sat there groaning, head bowed, eyelids clenched in pain. "Ren," he mumbled, "I don't know what you're talking about . . . but I'll try anything. Whatever it is, just do it."

Without further comment, I laid my hands on his head and by the authority of the holy priesthood invoked a blessing from the Lord. The words came spontaneously with total conviction, as though my wounded comrade and I were united by some vibrant power much like the force of a great electromagnet. Never had I felt the power of the priesthood so greatly. Mitch would recover; that I knew for a certainty.

Two days later Mitch Spencer astounded and dismayed doctors in Livingston by leaving the hospital on his own power. Two weeks after that he was again hunting lions.

So I had learned firsthand years before that God could preserve life in the midst of all the dangers of Africa. We would return and finish the work we had been called to do.

CHAPTER NINETEEN

Onward, Christian Soldiers

Saying farewell to our beloved companions, Ted and Janath, had been hard, but Ghana was once more open to travel, and it seemed essential that we now have someone there permanently. Having received approval from Church headquarters, they had set forth smiling, bravely refusing to articulate the trepidation we all felt in our hearts. One lone missionary couple per country! How would it ever be possible to carry on the work, even to simply maintain the strongholds already established?

Undoubtedly the Brethren were doing their best to obtain reinforcements, but married couples with the right qualifications were apparently hard to find. Frank and Clora Martin, the only other couple called thus far, were having visa problems and would not be arriving as scheduled. This seemed ironic in light of our understanding that future missionaries would be able to obtain visas far more easily than we had, the kind that would likely be in force for one or two years. The establishment of districts and branches with leaders who could write favorable letters to the capital in Lagos and the Nigerian Embassy in Washington had made such an assumption reasonable.

But for now it was more of the old waiting game—and wait we did, not only for the Martins, but much of the time for almost everything related to our daily existence. We had now entered the rainy season with its blessed relief from the heat, yet culinary water was scarcer than ever because the city intakes were frequently clogged with sand as a result of the flooding. Our home was without any water for days on end, and at times, having been compelled to share the same bath water, we left it in the tub—something with which to flush the toilet. "You know," I remarked, "merely seeing that toilet flush has become an experience of epic proportions."

Rachel laughed, then shook her head morosely. "Seriously, is there anything worse than going without water?"

"Well, yes," I reflected, "having too much. Just ask someone who has been alone in the ocean—out there in the middle somewhere without anything to keep him afloat." On days when it stormed, however, I sought the deluge. Wrapping myself in a towel and grabbing a bar of soap, I would hasten outside and stand under the gushing rainspout. Utter revelry!

The Martins had originally been scheduled to arrive in Enugu on June 8, and despite the strong probability that they could not make it by then, we went to the airport. "Just in case," Rachel insisted, and I complied, partly perhaps just to say "I told you so," partly to bolster her morale. My wife has always been courageous, but it had been a time of growing hardship. She greatly missed her friend Janath, and no letters had arrived from home for days.

It was a period of trial for both of us, and I will always remember the look of hope on her face as the plane landed from Lagos. "Now, won't you be surprised," she said with a note of forced cheeriness, "if the Martins come right through that door!"

"Yes," I replied, "but I wouldn't be any more surprised to see President and Sister Kimball."

Sadly enough, we were not surprised in the least. No one even faintly resembling the description of our new companions appeared. The Martins were still on the opposite side of the world.

As we journeyed homeward I shook my head, trying to cast

off the mood of depression, "Aw, we've *got* to get reinforcements before long," I said. "One of these days they'll be coming by the dozens. Who knows? Maybe by the hundreds!"

Rachel looked at me, and her eyes began to glisten. "But when?" she implored. "No water, no mail . . . that I can take—but no companions! That's not *fair!*" And then she burst into tears.

I wanted to reach over and hug her, but the roads, as usual, were fraught with pitfalls. Instead, I merely patted her on the arm and suddenly burst into a refrain of "Onward, Christian Soldiers." My wife glanced at me a bit startled, thinking perhaps that I had flipped from the strain. "Onward, Christian soldiers! marching as to war, with the cross of Jesus going on before." Before long she began to smile a little and even tried to join in, but her voice was very faint, and it cracked like an eggshell. In order to compensate, I sang even more boisterously, and once the song reached its blessed conclusion, I gave her another pat. "Just think now—think for a minute what a lucky girl you really are. Exciting vacation for a whole year in Africa with one of the greatest operatic stars of all time!"

The tears were still coming, but my one and only for time and all eternity was laughing.

CHAPTER TWENTY

Alarms in the Night

At 7:30 in the morning on June 15, Rachel and I set forth for the Cross River area to meet with Brother Ime Eduok, the district president there, and visit several prospective branches. It was our first trip to that area alone and was rather uneventful at first. The journey between villages that evening, however, was another matter.

Never had I driven such treacherous roads. At one point we stopped in the gathering darkness to find the road completely swamped for the next fifty yards. It simply vanished into a large pond. We had parked with our headlights playing across the murky water, lights that blended with those of a truck on the opposite side, but before long a young man appeared and solved our problem. Wading out until the water reached his knees, he began directing traffic through the shallower part. It was a thoughtful act and much appreciated.

The following day we were a bit less fortunate. Approaching the village of Etinan, our car was lodged in a deep mud hole, with water coming almost to the floorboards. "You see," I said glumly, "there *are* worse things than too little water." It was an ideal set-up for the highway robbers we had often read and been warned about. Rachel made no reply—hanging in the best she could without complaint. Eventually, on the verge

Church leaders in Cross River State area (l. to r.): Edet John Ikpe, Bassey J. Ekong, Sunday D. Ukpong, and Sampson A. Ukpong.

of "abandoning ship," we gained enough traction to back out of the hole, and some helpful natives suggested another route.

From Etinan we traveled to Ndiya, where many people were gathered awaiting baptism. None of our priesthood bearers were there from the district or other branches, but the teaching and interviewing had already been performed over a period of several days by various branch presidents under the direction of President Eduok. One of his nephews, a bright young man named Ufot William Eka, did the interpreting for us. A short time later, at the Ndiya River, he was the first of his village to be baptized. I then confirmed him and ordained him a priest, whereupon he was promptly put to work, reading names off the interview sheets and witnessing the baptisms to follow. Upon becoming members, the next two men were ordained priests, the third, a deacon, and all of them provided much-needed assistance.

Our new deacon was quickly dispatched to obtain a stool for people to sit upon during their confirmations. A humble assignment, but necessary, and from small beginnings evolve mighty deeds and accomplishments. Now, in any case, we could go to work in earnest. As Brother Eka read off the names, our candidates entered the river, and I reached out, drawing them into deeper water by the wrist. Upon baptizing each person, I seated him upon the stool placed on the riverbank and proceeded with the confirmation. Meanwhile, Rachel recorded the names of our new members at a table on shore. Thus we continued from nine in the morning, hour after hour, right on through a short rainstorm during which one of our assistants opened an umbrella and held it over Rachel to keep the records dry. The final baptism occurred shortly after 1:00 P.M., bringing the total number of new members to 121. Quite an experience, and quite a workout for a man of seventy-one with a faulty heart!

That afternoon at the little plaster-walled meetinghouse in the village we organized the Ndiya Branch of the Cross River State District with Samson A. Ukpong as its president.

Back "home" in Enugu the work was also progressing well, and I was continually meeting new prospects within the city's business offices. Only a day or two after our return from Ndiya, I drove to our auto-insurance agency to obtain a new policy and was surprised to find our file ready and waiting on the front desk, clearly inscribed with the words, "Church of Jesus Christ of Latter-day Saints."

Smiling, I nodded to the young clerk seated before me. "You certainly give prompt service," I said.

"Thank you, sir," he replied. "I must confess, by the way, that the name of your church really interests me. Latter-day Saints . . ." he mused and peered at the words intently. "What does that mean?"

Once again, opportunity was not merely knocking—it was pounding. The moment I began my explanation all the clerks descended upon us with questions of their own, and seconds later the only other customer in the office tapped my shoulder. "I hope I'm not intruding," he said, "but I couldn't hear very well where I was sitting. My name is Jude Inmpey."

"Rendell Mabey," I replied, and reached for his extended hand. "I'm happy to meet you, and you're not intruding in the least. Please join us."

All of my listeners were supplied with literature, and all of them eagerly agreed to attend our investigators' meetings. The name Jude Inmpey, however, will remain in my memory forever; it would soon become an inspiring part of Church history in that country.

By now our dreams of establishing a home branch in Enugu were becoming a reality. Thirteen people attended our priesthood meeting on June 24, with twenty-seven attending Sunday School and twenty-five in sacrament meeting. Lessons were taught and conducted by black priesthood bearers who also prepared and passed the sacrament. A wonderful, gratifying experience.

By now we had adjusted in many ways to our new living conditions. At least we were taking the difficulties in stride more easily, and our home was generally pleasant and comfortable. Our residence included the east wing of a duplex, the other wing being occupied by a Frenchman who worked for a local construction firm. It had no street number, was simply designated as Ekulu West, Plot 30A, and lay in the bend of a nameless dirt road. Heavy foliage and native crops including corn and yams covered much of the surrounding area, and our entire yard was enclosed by a six-foot high chain-link fence laced with barbed wire. Iron gates at the driveway entrance were locked each night, and two outside lights remained on during the hours of darkness.

Such precautions were commonplace throughout the area and, as we eventually discovered, highly necessary. "You should fire that night watchman," our gardener advised me one morning. "He sleeps on the job, and robbers were here last night."

"Oh, really?" I said. "How do you know that?" In reply he took me into the backyard and pointed to a large hole in the fence. Someone had definitely been at work with wire cutters, but a careful search revealed nothing missing.

"You were very lucky," the gardener said somberly. "Something must have scared them off. A lot of other people in this area have not fared so well."

That same day I had a discussion with our watchman, asking him to inspect the entire premises at least once an hour during the night and in general to be more alert. I was never quite certain how well he observed those requirements, but he later obtained a whistle and armed himself with a bow and quiver full of arrows. The arrows, however, lacked feathers, and I wondered aloud regarding their accuracy. "Oh, feathers are not really necessary, sir," he replied. "Allow me to demonstrate." With that, he let fly at a tree not far away, missing it completely.

So much for our sense of security, but our watchman had developed greater responsibility. One night several weeks later we were awakened by the sound of his whistle. Rushing outside, we discovered that two men had entered the compound. Caught in the glare of our watchman's flashlight, they had fled, given impetus, no doubt, by the fact that he was also brandishing a machete. Once again an opening had been sliced in the fence with wire cutters, and none of us slept very soundly the rest of that night. Rachel and I could not avoid recalling her recent conversation with a woman from one of the city's richer residential sections. The woman had appeared a bit careworn, confiding that she scarcely dared to leave her home anymore even with servants on hand. During the past few months five robberies had occurred within her immediate neighborhood.

In other parts of Enugu people had been rousted from their beds at gunpoint or with knives, and in some instances murder or rape had followed. In response, aroused citizens had begun forming vigilante groups, and robbers convicted in the courts of law were often executed by firing squad in public.

Robbers were not our only concern. On one occasion the gardener spotted a short, thick-bodied snake in the backyard, and before he could obtain a weapon to dispose of it the creature had slithered down a hole only fifteen feet from our doorstep. I concluded from the gardener's description that it was an African puff adder, one of the world's most deadly reptiles. Fortunately our night watchman eventually spotted the snake devouring a frog in our garden and killed it. Yes, definitely very poisonous, he affirmed—a puff adder. Needless to say, it was the last time we would wander about our compound at night without great caution and plenty of light. From then on, we literally had to watch our step.

Nigeria was also the home of the cobra and the mamba, both highly lethal, and both of which we had spotted occasionally during our travels. Ironically, however, neither snakes nor robbers were as menacing in the long run as the countless tiny creatures—microorganisms—never visible to the naked eye. Once each week we took pills to avoid contracting malaria, a disease carried by the anopheles mosquito. In addition, many of the ponds and swampy areas were infested with parasites that could penetrate the skin, evolving into blood flukes and causing a serious infection known as schistosemiasis. As a consequence, it was essential to select baptismal sites with care, shunning wherever possible water containing snails, which functioned as intermediate hosts for the larvae of these parasites.

Having become acquainted with Africa on safari, I understood its perils better than most foreigners did. "Remember, now," I often admonished, "we are in Africa and must never let our guard down." Our challenge, as I perceived it, was to be alert and prudent though never timid. The Lord's work often entails certain calculated risks—as indeed does earth life itself—risks that must be met with intelligence, enthusiasm, faith, and fortitude. In general, we had at least tried to follow that prescription, and in all our comings and goings we had been blessed mightily.

CHAPTER TWENTY-ONE

Help at Last

W ho's that little girl?" I asked. We had just pulled into our compound, and sunlight cascading off the hood and windshield made it hard to see.

Rachel squinted, peering from the window. "It's Lisa Knudsen."

Blonde, age thirteen, she stood at the end of our driveway, straddling her bicycle.

"Hi!" She smiled and gave a little wave. "My mom and dad said to come tell you the Martins are here!"

"They're already here?" Rachel's voice and expression combined jubilation with dismay—jubilation because reinforcements had arrived at last, dismay because they had arrived a day earlier than anticipated. We had fully intended to greet them at the airport, but fortunately they had managed to obtain a taxi and locate our friends the Knudsens. They were in good hands.

Minutes after Lisa's arrival we returned to her home for an introduction to our new companions, Elder Frank A. Martin and his wife Clora Carling Martin, a couple in their sixties who glowed with the Spirit and seemed like old friends from the first handclasp and hello. At the moment they were also very weary from long hours of travel and jet lag. Perhaps they were a bit disillusioned as well to learn that we had just been out in search of drinking water after eleven consecutive days without any in our home.

After the Martins had rested a little, Frank and I drove downtown for gasoline. While there we visited the post office to collect mail and discovered a cablegram that read: "Martin couple scheduled to arrive Lagos 5:55 A.M. Monday July 9 . . . arriving Enugu 9:30 A.M. July 9."

I shook my head. "We really feel sorry about not being on hand, but the last and supposedly final word on your arrival specified the tenth."

Frank smiled affably. "No problem. At least, we finally made it, and that's what counts." He had an affable face—dark, heavy-rimmed glasses like Ted's, but his face was somewhat heavier in the jowls and his hair was sparser on top. The face of a benevolent uncle or grandpa.

Yes, they had finally made it, and our new companions were certainly well qualified for their new calling. Frank had been an account executive in the San Francisco Bay area for many years, served as a missionary to England, been a bishop, high councilor, member of a stake presidency, and stake patriarch. His wife Clora had served in various Mutual and Relief Society presidencies and had taught numerous classes in all of their ward auxiliaries over the years. We had missed Ted and Janath greatly since their departure for Ghana some two months earlier, but our new companions would help fill the void.

Less than a week after the Martins had arrived, Jude Inmpey, whom I had met in the auto-insurance agency, was baptized and confirmed. Others to become members of the Church along with him were his wife, Mary-Emelda, and a young man named Benedict Paul Onwuatuegwu, long confined to a wheelchair. That same day the Enugu group became a branch, with Paul O. A. Ihuoma as president, Wilfred C. Okenchi and Jude I. Inmpey as counselors, Hyginus S. Chukwu as clerk, and Harold Iwuoh as Sunday School president. The dream of a home branch in Enugu had become a tangible reality under the direction of powerful, dedicated leaders, men of great spirituality and understanding.

Meanwhile, however, many of the branches we had established elsewhere were in growing need of attention. On July

Elder Mabey and Enugu Branch presidency (l. to r.): Hyginus S. Chukwu, clerk; Paul O. A. Ihuoma, president; Wilfred C. Okenchi, first counselor; (extreme right) Jude I. Inmpey, second counselor. Second from right is Harold E. Iwuoh, branch Sunday School president.

20, we received three letters from our Nigerian Saints and one from an investigator, each of which left us feeling rather frustrated and disconsolate. Although the tone in each case was that of humility, feelings of being neglected were also obvious.

A letter from Brother John Owugah, one of four members baptized in a remote village the preceding January, was truly heart-wrenching. "You came and went back on the day of baptism," he wrote. "We did not see you and Brother Cannon again. Since then I have been asking of you all; the Church is not progressing well because of no Church building here. We have so many people who will like to be baptized in the name of God . . . and I am waiting anxiously for your reply."

Another from Brother Ime Eduok, president of the Cross River State District, warned, "The work in Cross River State is going to suffer the more because of lack of knowledgeable men in the gospel to teach the churches already organized." President Eduok went on to explain that his car had broken down and that it would be impossible for him to fulfill his calling without proper transportation. He exhorted us to send more missionaries and offered to lodge them in his own home if we could advance him funds to complete additional construction then underway.

A prison guard, B. B. Excellsior, living on the coast of Cross River State, had also written informing us of his growing desire for baptism and his hope that it might be accomplished during his annual leave in the near future. Transportation was a real problem, he said, but he was convinced that he could help establish churches throughout the area if we could provide him with a motorcycle.

"That gives you some idea of the challenge we face," I told the Martins. "At the barest minimum, we need three additional missionary couples here in Nigeria and could easily use many more. The same is true for Ghana."

They nodded gravely. "And I suppose," Clora observed, "that it's pretty difficult finding couples with the necessary temperament and background."

"I would imagine, too, that there's a certain amount of reluctance in most cases regardless," Frank said. "They told us this would be a real hardship mission in some ways, and from what you've said—what we've already observed, in fact —that's correct. I guess the whole thing can be a little scary for older couples, especially those with any health problems." We did not realize then that he had undergone a hip replacement or that Clora suffered from migraine headaches and back trouble, conditions that could have undoubtedly provided them an easy "out" had they desired it.

"It really is difficult in some respects," Rachel admitted. "Occasionally I've felt pretty depressed, wondered if we could endure to the end or not. At the same time, I realize that we must have it very easy compared to what many of the early missionaries faced, and the blessings are so tremendous."

"That's right," I said. "If people could only realize the magnificence of this mission, the miracles that happen almost every day, these so-called hardships wouldn't have much significance."

CHAPTER TWENTY-TWO

The Harvest Is Great

A day later, spurred on in part by the letters just received, we headed for Cross River State and a meeting with President Ime Eduok in the village of Uyo. Among other things, I was concerned about the accuracy of our membership records and feared, in fact, that the Church might always have problems in that regard. In many cases, the Nigerians themselves cannot tell a person's sex on the basis of name alone. Worse still, Nigerian names are not always officially recorded, and a surprising number of married women do not know their maiden names. To complicate matters, birth certificates are virtually nonexistent, and age is often determined on the basis of recollection alone.

Notwithstanding these problems and the great need for additional missionaries, despite our determination to proceed with caution, we found it impossible to refuse baptism to those who were truly ready and waiting. Thus, on July 22, only two weeks after their arrival, our new companions gained an idea of what the harvest could be like in Black Africa. That day Elder Martin and I were privileged to baptize and confirm 115 people from three villages in the Cross River State District and organize a new branch.

At seven that evening, we spoke at a meeting of the Spiritual Holiness Church in Etinan as a result of letters exchanged with its pastor, L. U. Nsa, some time earlier. As so often happened on such occasions, we were royally welcomed—loudly, too, thanks to the pounding of native drums. The official address by Pastor Nsa began as follows:

"Beloved Brothers and Sisters in Christ:

"We, the members of the Spiritual Holiness Church are happy to welcome you into our small, brotherly, love abiding and oneness-of-purpose centre. Your maiden visit to us has come at the right time when we are zooming about in search of a true earthly spiritual leadership. As God chose Moses to free the Israelites from the bondage of Pharaoh and made them the inheritance of the promised land after much suffering and wandering in the Wilderness for 40 (forty) years, it is therefore our firm belief that God has chosen you as our leader to free us from earthly limitations and lead us to inherit that land prepared by God for his Saints everywhere."

The same address was presented to us in written form afterward, signed by the good pastor and six other church officials. One could hardly ask for a more positive greeting, and all that "zooming about" was to soon be rewarded in a big way. Before leaving, we presented our new friends with copies of the Book of Mormon, the Doctrine and Covenants, and other Church literature. They reciprocated with a live chicken, eggs, and several large yams. We then drove off into the night having arranged with those who could read to teach the material provided and for all involved to study the gospel under the direction of our branch presidents in that area. A baptism would be held several weeks hence for those worthy and prepared.

Returning to Enugu the following day, we came to a bridge that was under repair. Workers were tearing out the old, decayed planking, and vehicles were soon backed up behind us for some distance. "Well," I said, "nice to have that bridge made safe at last, but what do we do in the meantime? Looks as if we're in for a wait of several hours."

"Or longer," Frank said dubiously. "Could be a whole day or more the way it looks from here."

Leaving our car, I approached the crew foreman and asked him how long we might be delayed. "We are missionaries of The Church of Jesus Christ of Latter-day Saints," I explained, "and must return to Enugu before dark."

The foreman nodded, staring at the ground. "In that case," he said thoughtfully, "we must allow you to pass." Then he looked up and grinned. "Provided, of course, you are willing to supply us with some of your Church literature."

"Gladly," I said, and I did as requested. The foreman then signaled his crew, directing them to replace enough planks for a precarious crossing, and before long we were on our way. The only other vehicle allowed to pass was the taxi just ahead that had been blocking our way.

Later that afternoon we encountered a roadblock where a new highway was under construction, almost ready for use. A security captain was sitting in a truck nearby, however, and the moment I informed him that we were missionaries, he instructed the guard to let us pass. The price? More Church literature—our ticket to a new, smooth highway, a splendid, traffic-free journey almost all the way home.

Upon first arriving in Nigeria, we had been cautious about identifying ourselves as missionaries, but it had soon become obvious that the title *missionary* was an honored one, the passkey to nearly every door, thanks to the work of other Christian religions that had come many years before.

The day after we returned to Enugu, the title came to our rescue once again when a garage mechanic informed me that the air conditioner in our car was badly clogged, that the cost of repair (like the cost of almost everything) would be high. Smiling a bit wearily, I said, "You wouldn't really charge a poor old missionary that much, would you?"

"Missionary?" The mechanic regarded me with interest. "Let me go find out." Moments later he returned to report that he had talked it over with his partner, who agreed that they should do the job free in the interest of their own salvation. "No charge to the Reverend," the repair slip read.

On August 3, after much delay, I managed to reach Elder Carlos E. Asay, president of the International Mission, by telephone, and was elated to learn that two more couples had accepted calls to Nigeria. They planned to leave the moment visas were available. Two more couples! We were literally overjoyed. During our conversation I ordered several thousand tracts, five hundred copies each of the Book of Mormon, *Gospel Principles*, and the *Family Home Evening Manual*. A big order, but so was the demand.

Elder Asay and I also discussed many important matters, including the need for a visit from Brother John Cox, Director of Temporal Affairs, headquartered in Birmingham, England, who had jurisdiction over Africa. Brother Cox, I stressed, could be of great value in helping us set up records on a more complete, permanent basis, developing a well-organized tithing program, handling other financial matters, and offering advice regarding the acquisition of meetinghouses. Thus far, because of continuing communication, visa, and transportation problems, we had been unable to determine a plan of action. I had, in fact, waited three hours just to place the phone call to President Asay himself.

In conclusion, we discussed the possibility of constructing small chapels in West Africa much like those being built in South America. It had become increasingly obvious that scattered membership and transportation problems in many parts of the world would necessitate building more chapels on a smaller, less costly scale than those we had become accustomed to "in Zion."

August 8, 1979, marked my seventy-first birthday, time for a little reflection, memories flowing back briefly to the days of my childhood in a small home of "dobie" brick there in Bountiful, Utah—the city where I still reside. Those seven decades truly had been *bountiful,* but nothing during that entire span could really parallel what was happening now. Suddenly I realized that we had little time left, only two and a half months. In consequence, I was sleeping less and less, often completing my journal well after midnight with only the chanting of insects and the croaking of frogs for company. Increasingly, I found myself awake and restless in the early hours of the morning, planning, pondering—puzzling over the best way to cope with the endless challenges. *Relax,* I would tell myself, *peace, peace, be still.* But my mind seemed to have a second mind of its own that refused to rest.

August 11 marked Nigeria's "Day of Destiny," one that brought an end to thirteen years of military rule as voters installed their first Executive President, Alhaji Shehu Shagari. More than ever, I could envision a time when the gospel would flow as living waters throughout Nigeria and Ghana, eventually filling the entirety of Africa. It was a thrilling conception, and yet one could never be certain what problems might arise. Among other things, I felt an urgent need to prepare our priesthood members for any emergency, to insure such stable, inspired leadership at all levels that the Church in those two lands could withstand whatever onslaughts the adversary might direct at it.

Our only black district president in Nigeria was Ime Eduok in Cross River State, whereas Roger Curtis and Bruce Knudsen, presidents of the Lagos and Imo State Districts respectively, were both foreigners like ourselves, residing there temporarily. Consequently, despite their excellent qualifications and dedication, I was increasingly uncomfortable with the situation and finally concluded that we should move toward native leadership wherever possible.

On August 15 we were visited by the Reverend E. O. Ukah of the Full Gospel Ministries. A handsome, dignified young man with a thick mustache, the Reverend Ukah had read *A Marvelous Work and a Wonder*, which we had given him earlier, and said he believed Joseph Smith's testimony. He had a number of challenging questions, however, and now desired to read the Book of Mormon.

During our discussion we were also visited by a young man living nearby who appeared to be highly agitated. Someone had given him several magic charms, and he was now convinced that they were evil. "I have tried to give them away," he explained, "but no one wants them. I have even thrown them into the fire, but they slither right out of the flames like snakes."

"Where are these charms now?" I asked.

"Still at my home, sir," he replied. "I don't know what to do with them."

I nodded soberly. Such fears were not to be ridiculed or treated patronizingly, and our guest was definitely very fearful. "Why don't you go back and get them?" I suggested. "I'm sure the Reverend Ukah won't mind accompanying you, and I feel certain that we can dispose of them safely."

The young man left with our friend and returned an hour later with the sinister charms bundled in his coat. The objects in question hardly looked threatening—two small medallions on a string, and a plastic tube containing strips of paper with words typed upon them. Incantations? I was never sure, but we made our way to the backyard and deposited them in a garbage-can lid along with the coat. It too had now supposedly become hexed or tainted.

By then it was well after dark. We had just doused the entire contents with diesel fuel and were ready to ignite it when the night watchman appeared. "Better not burn those things inside the compound," he warned. "It will bring you much bad luck."

I glanced at Frank speculatively, but he merely shrugged. "No sense courting bad luck," he said.

Moments later we lit our little fire outside the compound and watched it go to work. The flames burned furiously and within a few minutes had consumed everything in the lid, leaving only smoke and ashes. "Nothing escaped," I announced at last. "The evil objects are completely destroyed, and your worries are over."

The Reverend Ukah nodded and smiled shrewdly, almost imperceptibly, staring into the glow. "I'm reminded of how the believers in Paul's day came together and burned their works of magic," he mused. "Acts 19:19, as I recall."

Our young friend was now much relieved. His face was suddenly drained of worry, and before long he asked if it would be all right to visit us and study the gospel. Request granted.

The following week we had a pleasant, though disillusioning, surprise. At about nine o'clock in the evening a taxi entered our compound, and within minutes there was a knock at the door. There, accompanied by four suitcases containing all their earthly possessions, were Ted and Janath Cannon! "Chance you might have room for a couple of wayfarers?" Ted inquired.

"Come in, come in!" Rachel exclaimed.

"Yes, indeed!" I said. "Don't you know better than to knock on your own front door?"

Then came the handclasps, embraces . . . and also the introductions, for the Cannons and Martins had never met. The explanations came later as we visited in the front room. "So what's the story in Ghana?" I asked.

Ted shrugged, smiled ruefully, and shook his head. "They booted us out."

"Not exactly," Janath corrected. "They just refused to let us back in. I guess we told you about the women's convention in Nairobi. Well, the Brethren requested that we attend as representatives of the Church, but now we can't get a visa back into Ghana."

I leaned forward in my chair and sighed. "Ah me! Visa problems may be the death of us yet." But, even at that, it was a joy to have them back. So much to relate, so much to plan, so much to do. We talked together for a long time, deep into the night.

CHAPTER TWENTY-THREE

A New Record

During our sojourn in Africa we had been visited not only by Elder and Sister Faust but also by Victor L. Brown, Presiding Bishop of the Church, a good friend of mine for some years. Each of our visitors had been impressed with the miracle transpiring in Nigeria and Ghana, and Bishop Brown had spent four days with us. During that time we had discussed many vital matters concerning the needs of our people there and the status of missionary work. He had also visited several branch meetinghouses and future building sites in the Imo and Cross River states.

It had been a rewarding visit, and upon returning to Salt Lake City, Bishop Brown wrote as follows: "I can never tell you how grateful I am for the experiences I had in Nigeria. . . . As I said when I was there, I think you are on the frontier of one of the greatest historical events in Church history as far as growth is concerned."

Now, late in August of 1979, we were also visited by Elder Oscar McConkie, Jr., of the Church's legal department, and his wife, Judy. Brother McConkie had been sent to help us establish a firmer legal base in West Africa, and I spent several hours reviewing the contents of our file on that subject with him. Brother McConkie explained as well that he had arranged for law firms in both Nigeria and Ghana to assist us, and we were most grateful for his efforts in our behalf.

A short while later we welcomed our final visitor, Dr. Spencer J. Palmer, a professor of history at Brigham Young University and the author of many books. Brother Palmer had just spent a week in Ghana and had come on assignment from President Kimball to collect material for a book and also for lesson material to be used in missionary training.

Such company was much appreciated. It was consoling to know that we were not alone, that some of our leaders at home had seen firsthand what was happening. We were all crestfallen to receive a call from President Asay, however, stating that our "reinforcements," the Warrens and the Bartholomews, might not make it to Nigeria after all. Again, the mysterious visa problems, and by now we were honestly beginning to wonder whether they might ever be resolved. Truly, the harvest was great, but the laborers were few.

Our feelings were somewhat conflicting at times, but any disappointments were constantly assuaged by the blessings at hand. Although additional guidance was essential within each branch, we were also noting remarkable progress among our leaders. I often thought, for example, of Brother Anthony Obinna, president of the Aboh Branch, as the following excerpt from my journal indicates:

> God certainly moves in a mysterious way his wonders to perform. President Obinna was baptized Nov. 21, 1978 (only nine months ago)—the first black on the African continent to be taught by the missionaries, baptized, and given the priesthood. Now look at him—an excellent branch president! A credit to himself, his family, and the Church! A great leader!

In that same entry I lauded as well the efforts of Ime Eduok, president of the Cross River State District, for his great dedication and spirit. "How can the Church fail with leaders like these two?" I asked. "It will not!"

All throughout the area our black priesthood bearers were rising to the challenge with an enthusiasm that would put many of us at home to shame. I thought of the form letter distributed by Kalu Oku, leader of the Lagos-Bariga Group, encouraging his friends to learn of the Church:

Dear Brother:

This I have as an opportunity to extend to you the good news of The Church of Jesus Christ of Latter-day Saints which came officially into Nigeria in 1978. The Church was restored to the world by Jesus through the instrumentality of the Prophet Joseph Smith of the United States in the early nineteenth century. Now it has spread almost all over the world.

"If Nigerians would keep to the teachings of this church," Brother Oku wrote, "bribery, corruption, and other ills will be eradicated." He concluded by stating that the Church promised no material benefits, "only spiritual," and offered to visit those interested, in the company of "Church Authorities." At that time, black priesthood bearers were prohibited from baptizing and confirming except under our direct supervision—not because of any prejudice, certainly, or from a feeling that such brethren were incompetent. They were new in the work, however, and inexperienced. Without proper restraint we could easily lose control. Our large but orderly processions toward the waters could swiftly become a stampede without adequate preparation or record keeping.

Brother Oku had advised us in his letter that many groups in the village of Ozu Aban and vicinity desired baptism. Ironically, though, water itself prevented us from performing baptisms there for the time being—flood water. The service scheduled for September 15, only two weeks hence, would have to be postponed until the dry season in December.

As if to reinforce the fact, only one day after our receipt of Brother Oku's letter we were assaulted with a terrific cloudburst that transformed all roads and pathways into wild torrents. Always happy for a good shower, once again I donned my towel and hastened forth to a glorious, frothing inundation beneath the rainspout.

The following day was fast Sunday, and there in the little branch at Enugu we all shared a beautiful spirit. Wilfred Okenchi, first counselor to President Paul Ihuoma, conducted the meetings with great humility and effectiveness and was afterward ordained an elder. Jude Inmpey, second counselor, taught the adult Sunday School class on the subject, "Christ's Church in Former Times"—one of the best lessons I had ever heard.

Only a week afterward, this same fine and talented brother was to become president of the Imo State District, replacing Bruce Knudsen, who would soon be transferred by the World Health Organization to another area.

The day before, we had returned to the Cross River State District to set a new record in baptisms for a single twenty-four-hour period in the country of Nigeria. There outside the village of Eba, Elder Martin and I baptized 149 new members with help in the confirmations from District President Ime Eduok and Brother Spencer J. Palmer. These converts were former members of the Spiritual Holiness Church—the same congregation that had welcomed us with such enthusiasm a few weeks earlier, comparing our mission among them to that of Moses in leading the Israelites from bondage. Afterward we organized the Eba Branch with their former leader, Lawson Udo Nsa, as president.

The final month of our mission was now approaching, and rarely, if ever, had we been compelled to search hard for investigators. If anything, the search was becoming easier, a fact underscored by our record number of baptisms at Eba and a visit that same week with Paul Ihuoma, president of our local branch back in Enugu. "I have been discussing the gospel at length with some of the leaders in my former church," he said. "They now wish to join me in my conversion." He smiled at me conspiratorially, pursed his lips, and looked reflective. "And when that happens . . . no telling how many of my former congregation may follow."

I shook my head, incredulous over such a possibility, at the very thought. "How many members did you say were in your congregation?" I inquired. I had asked him that question before but wanted to make sure there was no mistake.

"About four thousand," he replied.

CHAPTER TWENTY-FOUR

One of the Valiant

On September 4 Ted and Janath were permitted to reenter Ghana with a two-week visa. Two weeks was certainly better than nothing, and we hoped that the time could be extended. Vain hope. Ere long they were back at our residence laden with baggage that was now becoming a bit travel-worn.

"This could get to be a habit, couldn't it?" said Janath.

"They literally expelled us," Ted added, "along with all the other aliens in that country." Ghana had recently undergone another military coup and the new government was highly unpredictable.

"Well," I said, "it's always good to have you close at hand, and with ninety million people here in Nigeria, we all ought to be kept occupied for a while."

A few days later the Cannons were off to the Cross River State District in a car crammed with supplies—food, water, filter, pots and pans, a hot plate, and a great quantity of Church literature. Much as they were needed in the country of Ghana, the demand in Cross River was just as great, and there they would serve the waning days of their mission. Meanwhile, we were without transportation in Enugu, but funds for another car had been authorized by the Church, and we planned to obtain one soon.

The Mabeys and the Cannons had now reached "the beginning of the end," a realization brought home to me very forcibly during a phone conversation with Elder Keith E. Garner, first counselor to President Asay in the International Mission. Two days earlier, he said, a meeting had been held with the Council of the Twelve to discuss missionary work and needs in West Africa. "Another meeting will be convened a few days after your return," Elder Garner continued, "and the Brethren are looking forward to your report."

"Well," I replied, "that will be a great honor and privilege for us, and I have a slight hunch we won't run dry before the meeting's over."

"I'm sure you won't," he laughed.

"Just so it doesn't fall on the opening day of pheasant hunting," I added—only half in jest.

Going home! Such mixed feelings. I scarcely dared contemplate all that we would have to leave behind us, including that close, spiritual companionship with the Cannons and the Martins. So many profound experiences together, so many challenges shared and conquered in so short a time! In addition to our missionary labors, we had spent the beginning hours of each day in study sessions, reading and discussing the scriptures at length, and we had faithfully held family home evenings every Monday night with few exceptions. All these associations had generated great feelings of love and rapport that had become a permanent part of our minds and spirits.

During much of their stay in Nigeria, Clora had suffered stomach problems and at times feelings of faintness. Nevertheless, she had persevered in the work without complaint. Clora and Rachel had taken delight in each other's company from the onset, talking and laughing together often with a special understanding. Both women also bolstered our morale with good meals whenever such preparation was possible, and I took occasional delight in snitching Clora's homemade cinnamon rolls hot from the oven. It was an indulgence, by the way, that I could allow myself without fear of adding weight. My suit coats, scarcely worn since our arrival because of the heat, now bagged astonishingly, generating plenty of laughter and ribbing.

Frank, in turn, had proven a fine and loyal companion to me. Good natured, humble, ever helpful, he promptly assumed the task of typing my official correspondence and keeping our bulging office files in order. All of us took sustenance from his moving and eloquent prayers, certain that his experience as a stake patriarch had taught him much in that regard.

By now we were feeling less alone in that great country. Often new acquaintances would stop us on the street to inquire how we were and to exchange pleasantries, and as always people were eagerly awaiting the glad tidings of the gospel.

It was a joyous time in many, many ways, but we were saddened to learn on October 2 that Sunday Daniel Ukpong, president of the Edibon Branch, had died after a long illness. President Ukpong had lived as one of the valiant, unswervingly dedicated to the gospel and earning a livelihood for his family under arduous circumstances. Unfortunately, the bicycle which we had provided him with the cooperation of our grandchildren had not come soon enough to do much good. Perhaps, however, it had eased his burdens for a brief season and helped him to know of our devotion.

Life at its very best is still full of contrasts—sorrow in the midst of joy, fulfillment in the aftermath of loss. During our last visit with President Anthony Obinna he had been confined to the hospital with high blood pressure, and we had given him a blessing. Later, having returned home, he wrote to us recalling his baptism the preceding fall, the beginning of a new epoch in missionary work:

> The seed of the gospel which you sowed will grow into a giant tree. The Church in Nigeria will surprise the world in its growth. The number of baptisms, confirmations, and ordinations you performed in this country show only a beginning.

"The priesthood blessing which I received in the hospital," he concluded, "has made me well." Truly he is one of the Lord's great stalwarts, and his letter arrived the very day that we had learned of Sunday Ukpong's passing.

A third letter had also arrived, this one from our daughter-in-law Louise, who wrote that the entire family was eagerly awaiting our return. Enclosed was a photo of our home and grounds in Bountiful, clearly well cared for, and I must confess that the scene gave us a twinge of longing despite the brief time remaining. In response, I wrote to each of our children, their spouses and families, thanking them for their love, support, and encouragement. All of them had shown wisdom and responsibility in managing affairs at home, and the awareness was very comforting. Whenever our time might come, Rachel and I could depart this world confident that our estate and growing posterity were in good hands, that the precepts we had taught would not perish.

Along with each of those letters to our children, I enclosed a copy of Anthony Obinna's latest message. "Here," I said, "is a missionary's paycheck—one which all of you deserve to share."

CHAPTER TWENTY-FIVE

Till We Meet Again

W elcome . . . welcome!" He stood there smiling, teeth white in the sunlight against his dark skin. A small man, compactly built, with an intelligent, friendly face that mirrored the words of greeting he had just spoken. The Reverend John Ogo Airiohuodion, founder of the Cosmopolitan Church of Nigeria, had been awaiting our return to Ekpoma for nearly two months. So had many of his followers—a membership involving about fifteen small "stations," as they were called, and possessing at least twenty assorted buildings.

The Ekpoma area was a part of the Imo District now presided over by Jude Inmpey, located in Bendel State about a five-hour drive northeast of Enugu, and our first visit had been an auspicious one. Having come at the Reverend Airiohuodion's urging, we expounded at length upon the gospel before quite a large gathering, answered many questions, left the usual literature, then departed, convinced that the Spirit had borne witness. In response, they had given us gifts—beautiful native robes for Frank and me, farming produce for our wives. "Your visit to us shall never be forgotten," the Reverend Airiohuodion wrote afterward. "It is the Lord's doing and is marvelous. I believe that God has already joined us together for the propagation of the good news of our Lord Jesus Christ."

Now we had returned as promised, and the Cosmopolitan Church of Nigeria was ready for its great transformation.

Leaving Elders Martin, Inmpey, and Knudsen to perform the interviews, I set forth with the Reverend Airiohuodion in search of a baptismal site and had a rewarding visit with him in the process. More and more, I was becoming impressed with his testimony of the restored gospel and willingness to follow its precepts regardless of the sacrifice. Once again I stressed that the Church did not provide salaries to its leaders, that in becoming a member he would lose his livelihood as a paid minister.

"I understand the situation," he replied, "but I feel certain that a way can be found to support my family." He went on to assure me that nearly everyone in the Cosmopolitan Church had accepted our teachings and that once we had baptized them the present houses of worship would still be available.

Eventually, after much searching, we found an appropriate baptismal site on the Orhiomon River about eight miles from the village. We then returned to assist in preparing for the big event ahead. Our service had been scheduled for eight o'clock the next morning, and we left for our hotel as night fell only to wander lost for nearly an hour along some lonely back road.

Returning to Ekpoma the following morning, we were surprised to discover that more interviewing awaited us. More converts had now arrived, some of them having journeyed long distances on foot. As a result, we did not reach our baptismal site until about three hours later, but then completed the service without interruption.

That day ninety-seven new members entered the fold, and, as always, it was a moving experience, though a bit different from usual in some ways. For one thing, many of those baptized seemed fearful of the water. Instead of relaxing as instructed, they would cling to us nervously, making immersion rather difficult. By the afternoon's end Elder Martin and I were both badly fatigued. All that clinging had actually left my wrist sore and bleeding.

One of the few people to undergo his baptism with real calmness was a professional photographer. Having taken a number of pictures at the request of people in Ekpoma, he handed his camera to a friend and strolled into the water wearing his street clothes. (Under primitive circumstances it was not always possible to obtain the conventional white apparel.) Like all the others, however, he had been taught, interviewed, and professed a strong testimony.

Many of those to enter the waters that day bore scarred designs in their skin, markings made with knife blades to designate their tribal origins. One older woman was virtually covered with these markings, as though some tattoo artist had been given free rein. Only a short distance from our baptismal spot was a juju shrine to the river god still well supplied with offerings of the harvest.

Superstition? I suppose so, by most definitions of the word, and many of the very people we baptized spoke a language that even President Inmpey failed to understand. Much of our communication had to be conducted through interpreters, yet most of the local leaders—men like Brother Airiohuodion— were well educated and enlightened. These, properly, became the leaders of our new branch even though formal education has never been a prerequisite for participation in God's kingdom. Desirable as it may be, that quality of soul called faith is far more vital, the ultimate key to an eternal education.

That day the twenty-fifth West African branch of the Church was organized in Nigeria with John O. Airiohuodion as President, John E. Ojelumese and Tompson Ogbeide as counselors, and Abraham Itua, clerk.

Only two weeks left, but the baptisms never abated. On October 9 two young men entered the waters at Nike Lake outside Enugu. One of them bore the scars of battle, having been wounded in Nigeria's civil war several years earlier, but that was all past now. He had emerged into a new existence rejoicing. "At last I know," he exclaimed, "why the Lord spared my life!"

We were accompanied that day by the Reverend E. O. Ukah, leader of the Full Gospel Ministries Church in Enugu. The Reverend Ukah had been on hand for the burning of those magical charms mentioned earlier and had visited us periodically since then with a number of challenging questions. At present he could not accept the doctrine of baptism for the dead, but he was still intrigued with our teachings.

Upon wading from Nike Lake that afternoon, I looked him in the eye and smiled. "Reverend," I said a bit mischievously,

At Etinan, missionaries and Cross River State District leaders
E. Daniel Ukwat, first counselor (left), and Ime Eduok, district
president. At right is Elder Frank A. Martin.

"last week I baptized a photographer in his dress clothes. The
man simply handed his camera to a friend and waded into the
water. I will now be pleased to baptize *you* in like manner
—just as you are."

Our friend was tastefully dressed in a coat and tie for the
occasion, and he chuckled, shaking his head. "Thanks, but no
thanks. Maybe some other time."

"All right," I replied, and clapped him on the shoulder.
"But you might as well give in soon—can't escape the truth
forever."

As we arrived at the car, the Reverend Ukah turned to me
grinning. "How would you like to ride back with me on my
motorcycle to Enugu?" he asked.

I laughed and shook my head, thinking of the treacherous
roads, erratic traffic, puddles and washes from the previous
night's rainstorm. "Thanks, but no thanks. Some other time,
maybe."

Five days later we arrived at Etinan in Cross River State for
a reunion with the Cannons. Ted and Janath had been hard at

work as always, having visited every branch and district and offered much-needed help and guidance. In several cases they had organized Relief Societies, and Janath had provided members considerable assistance in maintaining complete, accurate records.

It was an appropriate time for the six of us to take stock of the Lord's accomplishments in West Africa and to determine final priorities. By now it was apparent that Elder and Sister Martin would soon be all alone attempting to manage the affairs of what was now a full-sized mission. Despite every reasonable effort—letters and discussions with officials in Enugu and Lagos—we remained mystified over the matter of obtaining reinforcements. At least two more couples had been called, but visa problems persisted, and it was not until our return to the United States that I discovered a real bottleneck in Washington. A solemn, even frightening, responsibility was settling upon the shoulders of our dear friends Frank and Clora, but they faced it with fortitude and plenty of good, common sense.

Our meeting in Etinan, it turned out, was merely the prelude to a far larger one. President Ime Eduok and other Church members had organized a grand farewell in our honor and selected Etinan because it had a small stadium, apparently the only place large enough in that general area to accommodate the kind of gathering expected.

"I'm afraid Brother Eduok may have overestimated our popularity," Ted observed as we approached the stadium, but an impressive crowd was on hand as we arrived, and before long the seven-hundred-seat facility was nearly full. Many of those present, in fact, were nonmembers, among them a number of local dignitaries and chiefs.

The program was truly impressive, and all who spoke, regardless of religious affiliation, sounded like converts. One of the chiefs held forth with great zeal, maintaining that the Church should "go all out," letting those who had established Christian missions before us know that we were serious in spreading the gospel throughout Nigeria. A nonmember woman also spoke, stressing that our principles and practices were unique. "The people of Nigeria are grateful to those missionaries of the past who helped to provide us schools and

At the farewell at Etinan, Sisters Clara Martin and Rachel Mabey with two local sisters.

hospitals," she stated, "but those we are honoring today represent a practical religion that goes right to the heart of our spiritual needs and gives life a deeper meaning."

President Eduok himself proved to be an excellent master of ceremonies and delivered a special farewell address, copies of which had been printed and distributed to our many visitors. It began as follows: "Today marks a very important event for The Church of Jesus Christ of Latter-day Saints in Nigeria, and it will go down on record as a permanent part of our history in this state. We are sending off the pioneer missionaries of that Church in the persons of Elder Rendell N. Mabey and his wife, Rachel, Elder Edwin Q. Cannon, Jr., and his wife, Janath, who will all be leaving us shortly." His address then detailed the history of our labors in Nigeria, touched upon the bright future that he envisioned, and concluded with a strong testimony.

The entire meeting lasted some three hours, during which Ted and I were called upon to speak. In conclusion, the entire gathering arose to sing us a very special song. "God be with you till we meet again," rose the refrain, "by his counsels guide, uphold you . . ."

Can this really and truly be happening? I wondered. Where had the days gone? The year had come on bright wings like the flight of a magnificent, exotic bird, and now it was vanishing among the trees. "With his sheep securely fold you." Less than a year earlier, the Cannons, Mabeys, and the true Church were strangers in this locality. But now, all these people! Where had they come from? Their dark faces were luminous with the Spirit, with love—and they were waving to us. The pale color of their palms was like the fluttering of countless doves, and in their eyes there were tears.

"God be with you till we meet again. Till we meet, till we meet . . ." There were tears in our own eyes, and we waved in return, smiling, struggling to keep our voices steady, then failing without shame.

"God be with you till we meet again."

CHAPTER TWENTY-SIX

Take a Deep Breath

It was October 17, 1979—only three days remaining in our mission. I had arisen at four to continue writing an index for my ever-expanding journal on the work in Black Africa. By now I was well into the fifth volume, having penned some thirteen hundred pages. Who might read those pages in the years to come I wasn't sure, but I had developed the journal-keeping habit long ago and felt certain that it was more vital now than ever before.

Around seven I was in the bathroom shaving and listening to the world news over our radio when I heard a loud knock at the bedroom window. There was our local branch president, Paul Ihuoma, along with his wife and baby daughter. They had been knocking on the door for some time but failed to draw our attention at first because of the noise within. They had arisen early and journeyed some distance by public transit to visit us, fearing that Paul would have to work on the day of our departure.

"We brought you a little going-away present," Paul said, displaying a small wooden plaque containing the carved figure of an eagle. "All over the world people look to the eagle with admiration and respect. Many of us here in Nigeria also look up to you in like manner. We thank our Father in Heaven for sending you and want to present this as a token of our love and appreciation." It was a moving moment.

I later took Paul into our bedroom to see if he might like some of my excess clothing. Unfortunately, everything—the shirts, shoes, raincoat, overshoes and other items—was too large. I shook my head. "Don't feel obligated to take any of this if you can't use it, Paul," I said. "Possibly you can sell or even give it away, but maybe it's nothing but junk."

Paul smiled, then reached out and took me by the hands—a common token of friendship among men in that area. "A father should give his son anything he truly desires to," he answered, "and his son should always be honored to accept it." I merely nodded and gazed at the floor for a moment, unable to reply. The one-time "apostle," Dr. Paul O. A. Ihuoma. Now he bore a humbler title, and his immediate followers, once numbered in the thousands, were few, but they were like the leaven of which Christ spoke. His potential was now limitless, for he possessed a priesthood without beginning of days or end of years, the power by which worlds are created. And who knew, furthermore, the ultimate extent of his followers, converts to the restored gospel, within Enugu alone?

When Paul's father had dedicated him to the Lord years earlier, he had been touched with the spirit of prophecy, but he could scarcely have realized the full implications of that promise.

Our departure was still about fifty hours away, but the time of farewell was already beginning, and that same day a number of members came by. Among the visitors were Jude Inmpey and his cousin Emmanuel, both bearing gifts, and four members from the Aboh Branch, including Anthony Obinna's brother Francis. Unable to see us off because of heavy responsibilities, Anthony had sent his representatives with one last letter of gratitude, hope, and encouragement. They had made the three-hour trip without hesitation. "We wish you God's protection on your homeward journey," his message concluded, "and may God crown you with success wherever you are."

The final bonus for the day was a letter from our son Ralph informing us that we had a new granddaughter. "Oh, I can't wait to get my hands on her!" Rachel cried. Exultation, frustration, or both? Hard to tell.

"Typical grandmotherly reaction," I snorted and tried for a moment to feign disinterest. If the truth be known, I could scarcely wait either.

The remaining hours were filled with packing and the usual "finalizing," caught up like chaff and whirled away on the wind. Suddenly it was time to leave forever our dwelling there on Enugu's unnamed street. It was the morning of October 19. Brightly colored birds, two or three arrayed in scarlet, twittered in the long grass behind our dwelling. "I hope our night watchman will continue to keep the burglars at bay," I told Frank. "Make him earn his pay." The banana tree we had planted in the compound upon arriving there had grown astonishingly. In less than a year it had developed from a mere seedling to a young adult about fifteen feet high. Already it was beginning to bear much fruit.

We then headed for the Enugu Airport, accompanied by the Martins, Knudsens, and Cannons. Ted and Janath had just returned to us, having left the affairs of Cross River State District in good order. They would be taking a direct flight home and therefore planned to leave a short while later—our schedules returning us all to Salt Lake City at about the same time. Frank and Clora would fly with us to Lagos, however, for meetings with Roger Curtis, our district president there, and his family. They would also confer with various public and business officials regarding missionary activities and hold a baptism for sixteen more people before returning to Enugu.

The flight for Lagos was right on time, much to our surprise, and our good-byes to the Cannons and Knudsens were swift, hardly doing justice to our remarkable year together. "What can we ever say at a time like this?" Rachel said. Her eyes were moist.

"So much, there's no beginning or end," Janath replied. Her eyes were reacting strangely too.

"Hey," Ted chuckled, "we're all going back to the same place, remember?" Yes, only a matter of days, but the life we had shared as missionaries was over, and our farewell to Bruce and Ardis Knudsen was even more poignant. Who knew when, if ever, we would meet again?

No time, however, to philosophize on that score. Minutes later it was on to Lagos, the Nigerian capital, where we met with officials at the Immigration Office to discuss some continuing visa problems. Arriving at the Curtis home afterward, we were happily surprised to find Brother J.W.B. Johnson, our district president from Cape Coast, Ghana, awaiting us. He had come to see us off and also bid farewell to the Cannons a little later.

President Johnson discussed conditions in Ghana with us at length and conjectured that our missionaries would soon be granted reentry into his country. He had, in fact, filed a petition in Accra, the capital, requesting that the Church be granted a minimum quota of ten missionaries as soon as possible. "As always, there are many who wish to hear the message of salvation," he told us, "to become a part of this great church. Right now, in fact, I would estimate that at least seven hundred people are worthy and ready for baptism."

In many ways it seemed regrettable that our black brethren in both countries could not go ahead with baptisms at their own discretion, especially in the case of highly responsible and spiritual leaders like President Johnson. I was gradually becoming convinced, for that matter, that the Church was now firmly enough entrenched in West Africa to "go it alone" in many respects if necessary. Indeed, one of our great hopes had been to establish the gospel so firmly and comprehensively that it could roll forth there even if the doors should be closed to our missionaries forever. On the other hand, the need for an organized mission in those lands was immense, perhaps greater than anywhere else in the world. All that marvelous growth potential needed a methodical cultivation, lest it run wild. It needed resourceful husbanding by leaders with long and varied experience.

During our final twenty-four hours in Lagos the hotel had no running water. ("Just so we don't start taking the luxuries of home for granted too quickly," I told Rachel. "Besides, think how nervous you'd be if water should suddenly come gushing out at the mere turn of a tap handle.") Then, as the appointed hour drew nigh, we said our last good-byes—first to the Curtis family, then to our stalwart friend J.W.B. Johnson, who knelt with us in our little room to offer a moving prayer of thanksgiving for all that had transpired and a supplication for our safe return.

And finally—last of all—prayers, embraces, tears, words of love and encouragement with Frank and Clora Martin, those courageous souls who remained behind. "Well, old friend," I said and clasped Frank's hand. "You're in charge of the vineyard."

Frank smiled and furrowed his brow. "What a great vineyard!"

"But we feel so inadequate!" Clora exclaimed. "How can we ever possibly—"

"You can, and you will," Rachel assured her, "because you are the ones the Lord has chosen."

I nodded. "The right ones at the right time and the right place."

A short while later they left in a taxi to preside over God's work throughout the entirety of West Africa—fortified, we hoped, by the conviction that we would do everything possible to resolve the visa problem in Washington and expedite the arrival of more missionaries. Appropriately enough, the Martins were on their way to another baptism—one of those activities that *could* become habit-forming if one weren't careful.

Our plane left the Lagos Airport on the stroke of midnight. Once again we had become a part of the night and the sky. As with birth and with death, we had come from darkness into light and were going in like manner. Below lay western Africa, black as the fur of a panther with the barren reaches of the Sahara unfolding steadily beyond. Above us, the stars. Six hours hence we would land at daybreak in England. There we would visit Brother John Cox, Director of Temporal Affairs for Africa, and I would also undergo another check-up on my heart. It had ticked along remarkably well under the conditions. And who knows? Maybe it had even grown a little in the ways that counted most.

I pondered our forthcoming report to the First Presidency and the Council of the Twelve and for a moment felt somewhat apprehensive. I hoped devoutly that the Brethren would feel we had made the right decisions and not moved too rapidly, that we had launched the Church's mission to Black Africa in accordance with God's will. Much of the time, because of the isolated conditions, we had been on our own, but maybe that had been a good thing in some ways, for it had compelled us to rely on the Lord as never before in our lives. And yes, above all, I prayed that *he* was happy with our efforts.

"Well?" Rachel glanced at me from the corners of her eyes —those big hazel-colored eyes that flowed with such empathy. It was as if she had been reading my mind, and at that moment I loved her more than ever.

"Well?" I smiled back. "I can tell you one thing—the genie is out of the bottle, and there's no way under heaven that he'll ever go in again. We'd all better be prepared to accept that fact and respond accordingly."

I shook my head in disbelief. Would the sense of wonder never cease? I hoped not. "Seventeen hundred and twenty-three new members of the Church," I said quietly. "That's the grand total for Black Africa as of 12:10 P.M., October 22, 1979. Three districts and thirty branches in Nigeria, two districts and five branches in Ghana."

It was too much to assimilate, absolutely mind-boggling, and for a moment or two we indulged ourselves with simpler considerations—a glimpse of home and family. "You know," Rachel mused, "I had almost forgotten, but October thirty-first is Halloween." That was the day we would arrive in Salt Lake City following our activities in London and Washington.

"Say, that's right!" I said. "Should arrive just in time for the trick-or-treaters — *maybe* even a few little *Mabeys!*"

The jet roared with a deep and steady vibration, bearing us ever onward in its awesome power . . . and we knew now, more than ever, that all the praise and honor, all that had happened, belonged to God alone. Without his constant sustenance, without his Spirit to bear us upward, all our efforts would have come to naught. As well might we have hoped to surmount the earth itself that night by the feeble flapping of our own arms.

So much to ponder, so many feelings! Again I considered the irony of it all: Those who had waited so long for the priesthood, wanderers ever searching in the wilderness, had at last attained its fulness. Now, in their great spirituality and devotion, they might well lead the way for all of us. What an example—what an ensign unto the nations! For a moment or two it seemed as if I could hear the throb of native drums.

Within the world of my mind flowed sunlight and water, hundreds of beloved faces.

Rachel leaned back and closed her eyes, exhaling deeply. She seemed a bit tremulous.

My head inclined toward hers, our brows making gentle contact. "That's right, Sister Mabey," I said. "Take a deep breath."